Labour Legislation
and
Trade Unions
in
India and Pakistan

LABOUR LEGISLATION
AND
TRADE UNIONS
IN
INDIA AND PAKISTAN

Ali Amjad

OXFORD
UNIVERSITY PRESS

OXFORD

UNIVERSITY PRESS

Great Clarendon Street, Oxford ox2 6DP

Oxford University Press is a department of the University of Oxford.
It furthers the University's objective of excellence in research, scholarship,
and education by publishing worldwide in

Oxford New York

Athens Auckland Bangkok Bogotá Buenos Aires Cape Town
Chennai Dar es Salaam Delhi Florence Hong Kong Istanbul Karachi
Kolkata Kuala Lumpur Madrid Melbourne Mexico City Mumbai Nairobi
Paris São Paulo Shanghai Singapore Taipei Tokyo Toronto Warsaw
with associated companies in Berlin Ibadan

Oxford is a registered trade mark of Oxford University Press
in the UK and in certain other countries

ISBN 0 19 579572 5

Typeset in Times
Printed in Pakistan by
Mas Printers, Karachi.
Published by
Ameena Saiyid, Oxford University Press
5-Bangalore Town, Sharae Faisal
PO Box 13033, Karachi-75350, Pakistan.

To

ISHRAT

Ghazala, Saadia, and Haris

CONTENTS

Part 2: Labour Laws after Independence in India and Pakistan

FOREWORD

Mr Ali Amjad has authored a comprehensive text on the history of labour laws in the subcontinent and provided an equally dextrous analysis of trade unions in the democratic perspective. One would have expected nothing less from Ali Amjad who has combined his experience as a reputed lawyer and a committed trade unionist to bring us a book which will serve lawyers, academics and students with equal facility in gaining valuable insight in the laws governing the labour sector.

The author effectively traces the history of the labour movement and of labour laws to the advent of the British East India Company and provides a detailed examination of the first industrial legislation in the nineteenth century beginning with the Apprenticeship Act 1850. He gives an exciting illustration of the birth of the working class movement in the Subcontinent and the subsequent interaction between politics and the labour movement which culminated in the Trade Disputes Act of 1929 and the recognition of trade unions. The author concludes the first part of the book by analysing the effect of the First World War and the industrial legislation in the pre-independence period.

Part two of the book deals with the post-independence period during which, on the one hand, important legislation advancing the individual rights of the workers was enacted, but ironically enough on the other hand, the State curtailed the powers of collective bargaining and thus eroded the influence of trade unions as an instrument for advancement of worker's rights. The author emphasizes persuasively how the urge for economic growth for the privileged few has been propagated at the expense of welfare politics for the many and led to the advent of the much abused contract labour.

In his concluding section, aptly titled 'Looking into the Future', the author bemoans that the contemporary legal framework cornered the determination of disputes between workers and employers through statutory provisions in courts of law and left precious little room for a trial of strength between the contending parties in a traditional collective bargaining setting. The author refers to the new developments taking place in the name of globalization, privatization and liberalization and is alarmed that this may result in minimizing if not altogether dispensing with the welfare measure of the State in aid of deprived sections of the population.

Today the buzzwords of market place and economic growth are drowning out the need for an egalitarian social structure. The new economic mandarins say that there is no such thing as a free lunch and the workers will get what they deserve in the new economic order. But to my mind this is fairly meaningless when there is no level playing field or where the means to become 'deserving' are denied to the economically disadvantaged sections of society.

Ali Amjad has done an important service in collating historical developments of labour law and providing a cogent analysis. I am confident that this book shall engender a meaningful debate on the development of labour laws in Pakistan.

Justice (Retd.) Fakhruddin G. Ebrahim
Supreme Court of Pakistan

PREFACE

This work is intended as an introduction to the understanding of the main features of the labour laws as they have evolved during the last hundred years in this Subcontinent. Industrial law, or the labour laws as they are more popularly called, are of recent origin. They have come on the statute book, been modified, amended and grown along with the development and growth of modern industry, liberal democracy, concept of social justice and the Labour Movement. A study of the development of industrial law, therefore, of necessity, involves a tracing out at least in an outline, the growth of modern industry in the Indo-Pak subcontinent, as well as the movement of national liberation and social reform. It will also necessarily involve a study of the philosophies behind the socio-economic policies of the national leaderships of the Indian National Congress and the All India Muslim League and of the various Socialist and Labour Movements. After independence, the policies of succeeding regimes in the two countries and how they have evolved in practice and the changed perceptions in the recent years will also claim our attention. The collapse of the socialist states and its impact on the fortunes of the labour movement and subsequently on the trends of labour laws may require more than a mere cursory glance.

It has been aptly held by an eminent jurist Lord Hailsham that 'the law of one age can be the injustice of another'. To say that 'the law, if it was to last, had to adapt itself to social change' is only another way of expressing the same truth. The sociological theory of law, if we may call it so, is all the more applicable in the realm of industrial and labour laws. Its very development as a special field of jurisprudence is the result as well as an indication of the vast social transformation that has come about in the world, not excluding the South Asian

Subcontinent. A hundred or a hundred and fifty years ago, it was the law of 'master and servant' or the 'freedom of contract' which was relied upon to express the philosophy of law in the field of employer-employee relationship. This was indeed some advance from the time not very long ago when slaves were bought rather than employed with power of life and death over them rather than over their jobs and livelihood. The relationship between the master and the slave was one of status based on outright coercion—this was substituted under the new dispensation of an industrial society by a relationship of 'free contract' where a worker only sold his labour power instead of his whole body.

How 'free' this contract has been is described by Edward Janks in *The New Jurisprudence* in the following words:

...For some time after the disappearance of serfdom had practically changed industry from a status to a contractual basis, the regulation of industry was left to the provisions of private law, substantially the law of property and the law of obligations. This was in effect, the period of 'laissez faire'. If the mill owners operations fouled the stream, in which the neighbours had rights or if they emitted evil smells and raucous noises, his neighbours who suffered, could bring actions of nuisance against him. If a workman's wages were unpaid, he could sue his employer for negligence or any other recognised tort of the derelict subject in some cases to the awkward doctrine of common employment. But in the early years of 19th century, it became increasingly evident that the remedies of the common law were quite inadequate to protect either the employees in the industry or the general public against wealthy factory owners, who deliberately or negligently caused suffering and loss to them, and if the injured person ventured to invoke the law, sheltered themselves behind every legal barrier that a highly paid ingenuity could device.[1]

In the early days of *laissez faire,* the law of contract in the law courts and the law of supply and demand in the economic field was sufficient to 'take care' of all the problems in the industry. Succeeding generations of law-givers, however, candidly admitted that this 'equality' and 'freedom of contract' was more illusory than real. The contracting parties were hardly ever 'equals' and they could never really meet on an equal footing. The so-called 'freedom of contract' was rendered meaningless by the simple fact of life which was not merely of economic disparity between the parties but of total economic dependence, on the one hand and total economic domination and mastery of productive resources, on the other hand. The chasm of mass poverty was too wide to be bridged by 'free contract' which in the early period of industrialization could only be described as 'wage slavery'. This archaic view of the 'freedom of contract' between an employer and the employee found an echo in a *shariat* appeal before the Supreme Court of Pakistan when it was argued that certain impugned provisions of law amount to a contract between the government and the civil servants and this introduces free consent. The Supreme Court rejected the argument observing that 'in fact, it is not in the nature of a free consent between free agents. On the one hand State power is projected in the form of statute and on the other civil servant has no choice of a bargain on those provisions when joining service.' (PLD 1987 SC 304 at 339)

In our law courts and in the legal profession, we still hear echoes of 'common law' theories. All legislations in the field of industrial relationship are considered deviations from the principles of common law so as to be very 'strictly interpreted'. Translated in common parlance it only means that every possible means of avoiding the applicability of this uncommon law should be found which a 'highly paid ingenuity' could discover. The 'tendencies of the modern State', however, in the words of Harold Laski, 'run counter to the principles of common law' which has ultimately given way in the recognition of the necessity of State interference in the field of regulating the living and working conditions in the factories and numerous other aspects of industrial relationship. What factors have brought about this realization, or have assisted in this change would require a separate discussion elsewhere. For the time being, it may be sufficient to state that philanthropy or benevolence was the least important factor in liberating industrial relationship from 'Common Law'.

In his preface to the *Conditions of the Working Class in England,* Fredrich Engels, speaking of the effect of the French Revolution of 1840 writes:

> The Factory Acts, once the bugbear of all manufacturers, were not only willingly submitted to, but their expansion into Acts regulating almost all trades was tolerated. Trade unions, hitherto considered inventions of the devil himself, were now petted and patronized as perfectly legitimate institutions and as useful means of spreading sound commercial doctrines among the workers. Even strikes, than which nothing had been more nefarious upto 1848, were now gradually found to be occasionally very useful especially when provoked by the masters themselves, at their own time.[2]

Another factor in the economic situation, which led to the emergence of a more 'moral' industrial jurisprudence has been described thus by Engels:

> And in proportion as this increase (England's industrial progress) took place, in the same proportion did manufacturing industry become apparently moralized. The competition of manufacturer against manufacturer by means of petty thefts upon the working people did no longer pay...thus the truck system was suppressed, the Ten Hours Bills was enacted and a number of other secondary reforms introduced—much against the spirit of free trade and unbridled competition, but quite as much in favour of the giant capitalist in this competition with his less favoured brother. Moreover, the larger the concern and with it the number of hands, the greater the loss and inconvenience caused by every conflict between master and man, and thus a new spirit came over the masters, specially the large ones which taught them to avoid unnecessary squabbles, to acquiesce in the existence and power of trade unions.

The growth and development of industrial jurisprudence is thus a part of the process of social changes reflected in the *juris corpus* of every community. Julian Huxley's remarks in his essay 'Economic man and Social man', would bear some lengthy reproduction:

> Many of our old ideas must be retranslated, so to speak, in a new language. The democratic ideas of freedom, for instance, must by its meaning of individual liberty in the economic sphere, become adjusted to new conception of social duties and responsibilities. When a big employer talks about his democratic right of individual freedom, meaning thereby a claim to socially irresponsible control over a huge industrial concern and over the lives of tens of thousands of human beings that he happens to employ, he is talking in a dying language.

As observed by the Supreme Court of Pakistan, 'the task of an Industrial Court in adjudicating and determining industrial disputes is not to discover what the rights of the parties are, under an existing contract of service. It really extends to the making of a new contract, limited only by the general principles of what is in keeping with equity and good conscience.' Equity and good conscience, however, reflect the social attitudes of the judges no less than the prevailing public opinion. It is here therefore that the question of what is social justice assumes importance. That the concept does undergo sometimes a fundamental change and sometimes a change of emphasis need not be gainsaid. All this depends upon the period, the communities and the countries we are dealing with at a particular time.

This adaptation of law to the imperatives of social change has been a difficult and often tortuous process in all the countries of the world. More often than not, bloody revolutions and acute political conflicts have resolved the conflict between the laws of a bygone age and the requirements of an emerging social order. An entirely new system of laws replaced the old where an older political regime was completely overthrown, as in the French or the Russian revolutions. In other places and at other times, the problem has been more complex. As in most of the Third World countries, the new post-colonial regimes were more or less peaceful and pliant successors to the earlier regimes, inheriting the earlier social and legal order. The process has been slow, sometimes, too slow to make immediate impact. But even in these countries, the setting of new social objectives and adoption of the legal system to these objectives and priorities has not come about without serious social and political tensions and often conflicts between the legislature and the judiciary, and sometimes between an assertive public opinion and an antiquated ruling class and its legislative organs.

An effort will be made in the following pages to trace out the changing concepts of industrial jurisprudence and the philosophy behind the emerging and developing industrial laws in the colonial and post-colonial period in this Subcontinent. In Pakistan, the development of labour laws and the policies underlying the various enactments have a rather confusing history and sometimes conflicting motivations can be discerned. It is not always easy to see a consistent pattern behind the spate of legislations in the course of last fifty years. The only thing that can possibly be said is that the course of industrial legislation has been as tortuous and uncertain as the course of Pakistan's politics.

Since 1990, the law of industrial relations appears to be entering a new phase with the policy of 'privatization' and 'liberalization' becoming more in vogue, minimizing if not altogether dispensing with the 'welfare measures' of the State in aid of the deprived sections of the population. What remains to be seen is whether the replacement of welfare industrial legislation by *laissez faire* in industrial relationship leads to more social conflict or less. The dominant trend in the official circles, at least in this country, at the turn of the century appears to be for more restrictive legislative and administrative action against the trade unions and less of ameliorative and welfare measures. In the opinion of this writer, these strands are likely to further accelerate social tension. The myth that pursuit of pure self-interest by every body, à la Adam Smith, with no holds barred, will lead to the greatest good for the greatest number is not shared by all in this country and not borne out by the recent history of globalization in East Asia and other parts of the world.

NOTES

1. Edward Janks, *The New Jurisprudence*, p. 251.
2. Fredrich Engles, *Conditions of the Working Class in England*, Preface.

PART 1

LABOUR LEGISLATION DURING THE BRITISH RULE

1 ADVENT OF BRITISH EAST INDIA COMPANY

Sociologists and economic historians have divided the 200 years or so of British rule in India into three periods. The first period commencing from the Battle of Plassey in 1757 to around 1813, is associated with the monopoly of East India Company in the India and China trade, which has been properly called the period of merchant capital. G.D.H. Cole in his book, *Introduction to Economic History (1757-1857)*, writes:

> This capitalism of two centuries ago was in many ways very unlike the capitalism of today, but it was based, for the most part, not on the direct employment of large number of workers in factories but on the large scale control by merchants of the buying and selling of goods made under conditions of small scale production. The typical capitalist of the eighteen century was the commercial man and above all the merchant engaged in foreign trade. The great joint stock concerns of the time were, in the main, not industrial enterprises but trading ventures, such as the East India Company. The way to get rich was not primarily by making things but by buying them from those who made them and re-selling them at a profit. Merchant capitalism came into being before industrial capitalism, which became the dominant system only with the advent of the machine age.[1]

The original aim of the East India Company in its trade with India was the typical aim of the monopolist companies of merchant capital to make a profit by securing a monopoly trade in the goods and products of an overseas country. The governing object was not the hunt for a market for British manufactures but the endeavour to secure a supply of the products of India and East Indies (spices, cotton goods and silk goods) which found a ready market in England and Europe and could yield a rich profit on every successful expedition that returned with a supply. The period of merchant capital quite naturally is a period of charters and grants of the Sovereign to carry on sea trade with distant countries—an operation which is trade only in name and is more of a high sea piracy and forays on African coast for the capture of slaves, which in turn 'generated' the capital necessary for purchasing of goods in countries, where it could not be straight away plundered and pirated. The period of modern industry proper had not yet arrived, nor had the period of labour legislations. The law that prevailed was of the 'master and the slave' which only very much later came to be modified as the law of the 'master and the servant'.

The peculiarity of development in India under the aegis of its British masters was that before India could embark upon any sizeable industrialization in the modern sense of the term, and before the industrial revolution could 'arrive' in this country, it was preceded by an unprecedented destruction and demolition of the then existing base of industrial production. Rajni Palme Dutt in his book *India Today* has rightly noticed that while in England, the ruin of the handloom weavers was accompanied by the growth of the new machine industry, in India the ruin of millions of artisans and craftsmen was not accompanied by the growth of any machine industry. The old populous manufacturing towns like Dacca (now Dhaka) and Murshidabad (which Clive had described in 1751 to be as extensive, populous and rich as the city of London), Surat and the like were in a few years rendered desolate under the *pax Britannica* with a completeness which no ravages of the most destructive war or foreign conquest could have accomplished. In the parliamentary enquiry in 1840, Sir Charles Trevelyan testified that 'the population of Dacca had fallen from 150,000 to 30,000 or 40,000 and that jungle and malaria are fast encroaching upon the town— Dacca which was the Manchester of India has fallen off from a very flourishing town to a very poor and small one. The distress there has been very great indeed.'[2] Montgomery Martin, the early historian of British empire in the same enquiry states 'the decay and destruction of Surat or Dacca or Murshidabad and other places where native manufacture was carried on is too painful a fact to dwell upon. I do not consider that it has been in the fair course of trade; I think it has been the power of the stronger exercised over the weaker.'

Sir Henry Cotton writes in 1890,

Less than 100 years ago the whole commerce of Dacca was estimated at ten million (10,000,000) of rupees and its population at 200,000. In 1787 the exports of Dacca muslin to England amounted to 3 million (3,000,000) of rupees. In 1817 they had ceased altogether. The arts of spinning and weaving which for ages afforded employment to a numerous and growing industrial population, have now become extinct, families which were formerly in a state of affluence have been driven to desert the towns and betake themselves to the villages for a livelihood. This decadence had occurred not in Dacca only but in all districts. Not a year passes in which commissioners and district officers do not bring to the notice of Government that the manufacturing classes in all parts of the country are becoming impoverished.[3]

According to H.H. Wilson:

The method of operation of the East India Company was to forcibly take away the goods and commodities of the peasants, merchants etc. for a fourth part of the value and to force the *Rayets* to pay five rupees for goods which were worth no more than one rupee. They arbitrarily decided what quantities of goods each manufacturer shall deliver and the prices at which he shall sell them. The assent of the poor weaver was in general not deemed necessary. For the *Gomastha* when employed on the Company's investment, frequently made them sign what they pleased and upon the weavers refusing to take the money offered, it has been known that they have been sent away with flogging. A number of these weavers were generally also registered in the books of Company's *Gomastha* and not permitted to work for any others, being transferred from one to another as so many slaves. The roguery practiced in this department is beyond imagination, but it all terminates in defrauding of the poor weaver, for the prices which a Company's *Gomasthas* in confederacy with the *Jachenders* (examiners of fabrics) fix upon the goods are in all cases at least 15 per cent and sometimes even 40% less that the goods so manufactured would sell in public bazaar or market upon free sale.

This plunder of the Indian weaver or the Indian handloom manufacturer had made the Indian goods so cheap that in 1813 the cotton and silk goods of India could be sold for a profit in the British market at a price from 50 per cent to 60 per cent lower than those fabricated in England. It consequently became necessary to protect the latter by duties of upto 70 per cent and 80 per cent of the value or by positive prohibition. Had this not been the case, had not such prohibitory duties been imposed by the State in Great Britain, the mills of Paisley and Manchester could have been stopped in their outset and could scarcely have been again set into motion even by the power of steam. They were created by the sacrifices of the Indian manufacturer.[4]

Destruction of the Indian handicraft industry thus proceeded in two ways. In the initial stage, corresponding to the period of merchant capital when modern industry in England had not yet come up, the plunder of Indian agriculture and of the Indian handicraft manufacturer brought to the British industry the much needed flow of cash capital on the basis of which the British industry was set up. Later when Manchester and other centres of British cotton industry developed as the result of the Industrial Revolution, the destruction of the Indian manufacture came about by completely closing the market for these goods in Europe and in England and even physically eliminating the handloom weaver, craftsmen and his industry.

W. Cunningham in his work, *Growth of English Industries and Commerce in Modern Times* graphically describes the role played by the Indian Empire of Britain:

Plassey was fought in 1757 and probably nothing has ever equalled the rapidity of the changes which followed. In 1760, the flying shuttle appeared and coal began to replace wood in iron industry. In 1764, Hargreaves invented the spinning jenny, in 1776 Crompton contrived the Mule, in 1785 Cartwright patented the power loom and above all in 1768 what matured was the steam engine, the most perfect of all means of centralizing energy. But though these machines served as outlets for the accelerating movement of the time, they did not cause that acceleration. In themselves inventions are passive, many of the most important having remained dormant for centuries, waiting for sufficient 'store of force' to be accumulated to set them working. That 'store' was in the shape of money and money not hoarded but in motion. Before the influx of the Indian treasure and expansion of trade which followed, no force sufficient for these purposes existed and had Watt lived fifty years earlier, he and his invention must have perished together. Possibly, since the world began, no investment has ever yielded the profit reaped from the Indian plunder, because for nearly fifty years Great Britain stood without a competitor. From 1694 to Plassey in 1757 the growth had been relatively slow. Between 1760 and 1815 the growth was very rapid and prodigious.[5]

The plunders of the East India Company in this first phase to purchase the goods manufactured by Indian craftsmen at nominal prices and sell them at fabulous prices in England and Europe; and the total destruction of the Indian manufacturing industry in the second phase was the economic foundation of their rule laid by the British law-givers in India. The phase did not call for any 'legislation' in the economic field or in the field of industrial relations and there were none, because the final arbiter, the naked use of force was the only 'legislation' enacted.

NOTES

1. G.D.H. Cole, *Introduction to Economic History (1757-1857)*, London: Macmillan, 1952, p. 32.
2. Parliamentary Enquiry of 1840 cited by R. Palme Dutt in *India Today*, p. 120.
3. Cited by Rajni Palme Dutt in *India Today*, p. 120.
4. H.H. Wilson, *History of British India*, vol. 1, p. 385.
5. W. Cunningham , *Growth of English Industries and Commerce in Modern Times*, pp. 259-60.

2 THE BEGINNING OF MODERN INDUSTRY AND LEGISLATION OF THE EARLY COLONIAL PERIOD

The East India Company lost its charter of monopoly trade with India in 1813 and from then on till 1857, it became a Company administering its Indian possession on behalf of the British Crown. In this process the Company also became engaged in expanding its frontiers and its powers over additional territories. The British Crown directly took over the rule of its most cherished possession only after the Great Revolt of 1857. To this period and till the end of the century, belongs the first beginnings of the modern Indian industry and quite naturally its industrial laws.

In 1813, for the first time, the British set up a cotton mill in Calcutta, known as Fort Gloucester Mills (incidentally still said to be running and now known as Bauria Mills). Twenty-five years later, that is in 1838, the Assam Tea Company was set up.

In 1845 two private British companies namely the Great India Railway and Great India Peninsular Railway Company were founded in London. Eight years later in 1853, the first railway line was laid from Bombay (now Mumbai) to Thane for a distance of about twenty miles. In 1857, the railway mileage had increased to 288 miles. But it was only after the Great Revolt of 1857, that large-scale construction of railway lines began in India, primarily to meet the imperial requirement of maintaining communication lines in the huge and sprawling country, which had come under the British domination.

The Bengal Coal Company had been founded in 1843, and the Jharia Colleries (in Bihar) came into operation only in 1857 to meet the requirement of railways. By 1879 there were fifty-six cotton mills employing nearly 43,000 persons, of which 75 per cent were situated in Bombay and twenty jute mills were situated in Bengal employing about 20,000 workers. According to Theodore Morrison, writing in *Economic Transition in India* (London, 1916), 'In the year 1880 to 1881 cotton mills, jute mills and coal mines employed 47,955, 35,235 and 11,969 operatives respectively. By 1905-1906 cotton, jute mills and coal mines employed 212,720, 144,879 and 89,995 persons respectively—quite an impressive expansion in absolute figures but not even a drop in the ocean of Indian humanity.'

The early generations of Indian men, women and children working in modern industries were subjected to as ruthless and revolting an exploitation as any known to the modern men. There was no limit to the number of hours a factory hand could be made to work. In the beginning, an average perennial factory worked day light hours that is eleven to twelve hours in the cold weather and fourteen hours a day in hot weather. From 1884 when electric light was introduced in the factories, the daily hours of work were increased from twelve and a half to sixteen hours in some localities.

Calcutta jute workers worked for fifteen to sixteen hours in the factory, besides two to three hours taken in reaching the factory. There were no rest intervals and even where some factory owners provided for the same, it was not more than fifteen to thirty minutes. Others did not allow any break and the workers were expected to eat while minding the machines. Leave was allowed only on some emergent occasions, which also required previous permission. There were no weekly holidays. The consequence was complete physical exhaustion of workers, who sometimes fell into deep sleep as soon as they had thrown the stump off the machines. Women also worked the same long hours as men until 1891, when their hours were fixed at eleven hours. The Factories Act of 1881 defined a child as between seven to twelve years and limited their working to nine hours a day. This was reduced to seven hours per day in 1891. But as can be imagined even these provisions were more often violated in practice. In Khandesh, children and women worked fourteen to fifteen hours or even sixteen hours. When working at high pressure, they sometimes worked day and night for eighteen hours continuously. To add to this cruelty carried out in the name of factory working conditions, the wages for such unusually long hours and back breaking work were paltry. The wages of cotton factory workers in Bombay ranged from rupees 7 to 20 per month. In smaller cotton gins and presses, it was not more than four annas per day for ten hours work.

THE FIRST ORGANIZED ACTION OF THE INDUSTRIAL WORKING CLASS

Corresponding to the first beginnings of modern industry in India, were on the one hand the first simmering of organized or sporadic actions of the working class and on the other the first series of industrial legislation, primarily intended to provide British capital a 'protected' and, in fact, a 'bonded' labour market. Only subsequently the labour laws became a little bit more 'moralized' as indigenous capital entered the field and posed a challenge to the metropolitan industrialist in limited fields of industrial production.

The strike of palanquin bearers of Calcutta in 1827 extending over a month was probably the first ever-recorded strike of transport workers. Its impact must have been similar to a strike of taxi drivers or tramway workers in modern Calcutta.[1] But we do not know anything more about it. In 1862, 1200 workers of Howrah railway struck work demanding eight hours work a day, presaging the demand of Chicago workers, of 1 May 1886, by almost quarter of a century. *Samprakash*, a Bengali journal on 5 May 1862 wrote in this connection:

Recently 1200 workers struck work at Howrah Railway Station, demanding 8 hours a day like locomotive workers for they had to work for ten hours a day. Work has stopped for the last few days. It is as well that the Railway Company fulfills their demands.[2]

A strike by railway clerks in that same year is also among the earliest recorded industrial actions by the upcoming industrial working class in India. Between 1862 and 1890 there were as many as twenty-five strikes reported from various places in the country. Revolt took place on the plantation and work was struck in coal mines. In 1895 an organization of jute workers called the Muhammadan Association was formed as well as an Indian Labour Union. The seamen in Calcutta and later the Goanees section of seamen formed their unions.

In May 1904, a general strike and *hartal* by Muslim and Sikh workers and railway engineering workers of Rawalpindi formed part of the upsurge in the Punjab which led to the deportation of Lala Lajpat Rai and Ajit Singh. Tens of thousands of Bombay workers went on strike for six days and staged violent demonstrations when Bal Gangadhar Tilak was sentenced for sedition by the British in 1908. The strike of British-owned East India Railway Company in 1906 was one of the most important strike actions sparked off, among other reasons, by a discriminatory wage policy, when the maximum pay of a first class 'native' station master was only Rs. 45 per month, the minimum pay of a Euro-Asian employee was Rs. 50 and of a European station master was Rs. 200 per month.

The first fourteen years of the twentieth century were also replete with strike actions of the oppressed industrial working class of India. Some of their organizations and actions were precursors of the wider national political movement that had started rising at about the same time under the banner of the Swadeshi Movement. As observed by the monthly journal *Swadeshi* at that time:

> Rail strikes were not caused by the Swadeshi movement but both the Swadeshi movements and strike actions were the products of economic distress prevalent in the country. Though the strikes were nothing new, their number, organization and political connections during 1905, 1908, made the period a distinctive one in the history of the labour movement.[3]

Despite almost universal testimony before the Commissions between 1880 and 1908 to the effect that there were no actual unions, many stated that labourers in an individual mill were often able to act in unison and that as a group they were very independent. The Inspector of Boilers spoke in 1892 of 'an unnamed and unwritten bond of union among the workers peculiar to the people' and the Collector of Bombay wrote, 'although this was little more than something in the air, it was powerful'. Sir Sasoon David said in 1908, 'though labour had no proper organization they had an understanding between themselves'. Mr Barucha, lately Director Industries in Bombay Presidency stated that 'the hands were all powerful against employers and could combine though they had not got a trade union'. Even though these statements were marked with a great degree of exaggeration, the British Deputy Commissioner certainly beat them all in giving a picture which was a complete travesty of truth when he said that 'the workers were master of the situation and the mill owners were really more in need of protection than the workers'. These half truths and sometimes absolute falsehood however did provide an inkling into what was actually a 'craft solidarity', the early beginnings of Trade Unionism.

THE FIRST INDUSTRIAL LEGISLATION

Corresponding to the initial phase of modern Indian industry six pieces of labour legislation may be noticed. These were:

1. Apprenticeship Act 1850 (Act V of 1850)
2. Merchant Shipping Act 1859
3. Workmen's Breach of Contract Act 1859
4. Employers and Workmen Dispute Act 1860
5. Indian Factories Act 1881
6. Transport of Native Labourers Act 1863 (amended in 1865, 1870 and 1873)

The Apprenticeship Act 1850 was 'necessitated' by the abolition of slavery, which was brought about in 1843. The Act enabled the pledging of Indian children between the age of ten and fourteen years for a period not exceeding seven years. It was made enforceable through a District Magistrate empowered to declare an Apprenticeship agreement valid and to impose penalty upon the party causing breach of the Apprenticeship agreement. No regular wages were payable to the apprentices until their adulthood. Thus the law provided a source of the cheapest labour which became in fact a means to effect the temporary pledging/enslavement of children by their parents or guardians under the compulsion of extreme poverty. This Act remained on the statute book until the promulgation of the Children (Pledging of Labour) Act 1933. Another device and one which was hardly concealed enabled the British capitalist in India to keep the Indian workers bonded and obliged to work for them in their factories or plantations on their own terms was the Workmen (Breach of Contract) Act 1859. Section 2 of the Act provided:

If it shall be proved that... a workman... has received money in advance from the complainant on account of any work and has willfully and without lawful or reasonable excuse neglected or refused to perform or get performed the same according to the terms of his contract, the magistrate shall at the option of the complainant either order such workman to repay the money advanced or such part thereof as may seem to the magistrate just and proper or order him to perform or get performed such work according to the terms of contract; and if such workman shall fail to comply with the said order, the magistrate may sentence him to be imprisoned with hard labour for a term not exceeding three months, provided that no such order of repayment of any money, while the same remains unsatisfied, deprive the complainant of any civil remedy by action or otherwise which he might have had but for this Act.[4]

In the year 1860, the Indian Penal Code was also enacted which came into force in 1862. Three sections of the Code provided for breach of contract of service under certain circumstances. The second report on the Indian Penal Code to the House of Commons stated:

> Some breach of contract are likely to cause evil such as no damages or only very high damages can repair and are also very likely to be committed by persons from whom it is exceedingly improbable that any damages can be obtained. Such breaches of contract, are, we conceive, proper subjects for penal legislation.[5]

Section 490 and 491 made a breach of contract under specified circumstances to be criminal like insubordination of seamen during voyage, desertion of post, negligence in the service of the master during a voyage, etc. However, of some greater significance, for the purposes of the present discussion were the provision of Section 492, which read as under:

> Whoever being bound by lawful contract in writing to work for another as an artificer, workman or a labourer, for a period of not more than three years, at any place within British India to which by virtue of the contract, he has been or is to be conveyed at the expense of such other, voluntarily deserts the service of that other during the continuance of his contract or without reasonable cause refuses to perform the service shall be punished by simple imprisonment/with hard labour for a term not exceeding one month or with fine not exceeding double the amount of such expense or with both unless the employer has ill-treated him or neglected to perform his part of the contract.[6]

Under the enactment, whenever a worker received an amount in advance in respect of his employment, he was bound to work for his employer for the agreed duration. In case of breach, the employer was not only entitled to the refund of money advanced by him but the worker was liable to be forced to perform the contract or to imprisonment up to three months. This was applied not merely in the tea plantations but also in varying degree to employments elsewhere. However, in 1898 and 1901 this law was replaced by the Assam Labour and Emigration Act, so that its rigours mainly came to be confined to the tea plantations.

Employers and Workmen (Disputes) Act 1860, empowered the Magistrate to summarily dispose of any dispute in respect of wages of workers engaged in the construction of railway, canals and other public work projects and for criminal punishment of workers who broke their contracts.

The second and third piece of industrial legislation of the period was the Workmen's Breach of Contract Act 1859 and Employers and Workmen Disputes Act 1860. It is interesting to reproduce the intention and purposes behind the Workmen Disputes Act of 1860 as stated in the preamble:

> Whereas much loss and inconvenience are sustained by the manufacturers, tradesmen and others in the several Presidency towns of Calcutta, Madras and Bombay and in other places from fraudulent breach of contract on the part of artificers, workmen and labourers who have received money in advance on account of work which they have contracted to perform and whereas remedy by a suit in the civil courts for the recovery of damages is wholly insufficient and it is just and proper that persons guilty of such fraudulent breach of contract should be subject to punishment, it is enacted as follows...[7]

There is ample evidence to show that all these labour legislations of the period, represented and reflected, the interest in the main of British investors and this continued to be so till the end of the British rule. Though the methods changed according to the situation in the different periods, the purpose behind these legislations remained the same. A reference to some case laws under the Indian Workmen Breach of Contract Act 1859 which was later amended in 1881, would be illuminating in this context. In the first reported decision of *CAA Vernede vs. Abdul Giri Hinna Swami*, the question arose as to whether a workman who had been sentenced to and had suffered imprisonment for failure to perform a contract for which he had received an advance, was liable to be sued in the Small Causes Court for the recovery of the sum advanced. The judge found that he had already been in prison because of his inability to pay the same debt. The judge thereupon referred to the Madras High Court the question 'whether the order of the Magistrate for re-payment of the money has been so satisfied by the subsequent CJ imprisonment of the 2nd defendant as to deprive plaintiff of his remedy by action.' Scotland and J. Frere of the Madras High Court held that the workman must pay, saying:

> The Act was passed for the purpose of punishing fraudulent breach of contract and imprisonment is the punishment provided for non-compliance with the Magistrate's order, directing either re-payment of the money advanced, or performance of the contract. In the former case the Magistrate's order ... remains unsatisfied ... if the money has not been repaid at the end of the term of imprisonment.[8]

Thus the worker who had no means to repay the so-called 'advance' now became a judgement-debtor of the employer who could get the decree executed by auctioning off all that the worker or his family possessed and civil imprisonment if the debt was still unsatisfied. Thus the employer now had a new weapon in his arsenal to make the labourer work on the employer's own terms under the threat of executing the court's decree, even though he had already once suffered imprisonment.

There were of course other decisions like the one in *Ram Prasad vs. Dirgpal*, where the judges took a more merciful view and prevented an employer from taking undue advantage of his workers' debts. The Magistrate dismissed the complaint of an employer who had advanced sum to his workmen to work as brass engraver holding that the Act was not applicable inasmuch as the money was not advanced on account of any work contracted to be performed, but was advanced as a device to keep the workers in debt so that they would not be able to leave the employer's service. The employer than petitioned the Allahabad High Court to revise the Magistrate's order. The High Court upheld the decision of the lower court. J. Oldfield said:

It appears that the money was given them as a loan, and without any reference to the wages or payment for the work they performed, which was to be paid for at a certain rate, without any deduction on account of the money they had received, and as a matter of fact no deduction from the wages was ever made. The money they received, therefore, cannot be said to have been an advance made on account of any work contracted to be performed; it was not to be considered in the payment for any work.[9]

The court further said that the effect of such a contract, if enforced, might be to give the employer the right to workers' services as long as the employer should be alive, on his own terms, as to wages and work. It, therefore, held that the Act did not intend to make the breach of such contract a penal offence, and that the employer could not invoke the Act against the workers.

In yet another case in Bhagvan Bhivsan, where a workman had contracted with an employer to work for him for one year in consideration of an advance of forty-five rupees but after serving for eight months had refused to work any longer it was held in appeal that unreasonable contracts could not be enforced under the statute. The District Magistrate reversing the order of conviction passed by the Magistrate said:

I think Rs. 45 was not a sufficient amount for the accused as a return for service extending over a period of twelve months; and in dealing with this case the Magistrate ought to have dismissed the complaint, deeming the unfairness of terms of the contract a reasonable excuse for neglecting to perform the contract.

The District Magistrate submitted the case to the High Court for affirmance. The High Court agreed with the order of the District Magistrate.

In spite of these decisions, however, clever employers could always write contracts to prevent workers from leaving their employment. *Queen-Empress vs. Indarjit*, clearly illustrates the situation. In that case, a worker entered into the following three-year agreement with the Elgin Mills Company at Kanpur:

> I ... agree that ... if within the period for which I have engaged to serve, I shall absent myself, or refuse to work, or take up service with some other... then I shall pay Rs. 99, the settled and fixed consideration, the Elgin Mills Company ... or the Company shall credit for the amount held by them as due to me, by holding me liable for the same, and I shall also be liable for payment of the penalty provided by Act XIII of 1859 on account of making any breach of contract in respect of rendering services entered in this document.[10]

The judge in appeal reasoned that Section 29 of the Act made a wilful breach of contract, without lawful or reasonable excuse, an offence, and did not require that such breach be fraudulent in order to be punishable. The rationale of the statute was explained by the judge in the following words:

> Consequently, I am of opinion, that this conviction was a right one, because upon the facts found there was most undoubtedly a wilful, and without lawful and reasonable excuse, neglect and refusal to perform the contract of service ... I need not point out the importance of statutory provisions of this kind, and their being enforced in large commercial centres like Kanpore, where by combined action on the part of persons employed in large commercial establishments there, the proprietors of those establishments might be placed not only at very grave and sudden inconvenience, but very serious pecuniary loss.[11]

Another decision of the Calcutta High Court dates back to 1881 under this enactment when an elephant driver (*mahout*) refused to carry out his duties for the master and was hauled up before a Magistrate and it was alleged that he had been paid Rs. 10 as advance. Thankfully for him, the Calcutta High Court found that the elephant driver was not a workman but a domestic servant. In 1926 a bench of the Bombay High Court dissented with this decision of the Calcutta High Court and held that Valta Bella Raut was performing manual duties while driving the elephant and this not only brought him within the definition of a workman but also within the mischief of the Workman Breach of Contract Act.

It may be useful to recall (and forestall) that 'personal service' in the eyes of the law givers, under common law was not found capable of 'specific performance', when it came to the worker or employee demanding restoration in service terminated for unlawful reasons. At a later stage, we shall see workers and other employees again and again facing the argument that though their removal from service was in violation of the terms of contract, equity as well as justice, no employee could be forced upon an 'unwilling employer' and that the Courts could not award the reinstatement of a wrongfully dismissed worker under the principles of common law or the Contract Act. But when it came to the 'unwilling worker' it appeared that personal service became capable of enforcement and specific performance by the use of compulsive methods sanctioned by 'due process of law'.

It need hardly be said that these labour legislations did not represent at this stage a 'benevolent legislation' nor did they in any sense of the term merit to be called 'welfare legislations', a terminology which is nowadays used to describe in general the labour laws. But a 'welfare measure' by the State is still regarded as somewhat of an anachronism, by advocates of liberalism as deviation and digressing from the chief function of the State which was to keep 'law and order' and protect property and profits.

FACTORY ACT 1881

About one hundred years ago the first Factory Act was put on the statute book in 1881. But this dealt only with the working hours of child labour. Mercifully, employment of children below seven years was prohibited and the working hours of children between the ages of seven and twelve were fixed at nine hours a day. The Act provided for some sort of fencing but nothing more. It did not mention women and men adult labour for whom there was no limitation on hours of work. Even such reluctant measure was made applicable only to factories using mechanical power and employing 100 or more workers. It specifically excluded indigo factories and plantations belonging to British planters from its operation and the hours of work of men and women were left unregulated. More factory legislations followed in 1891, 1901 and 1911. Under the 1891 Act, employment of children below the age of nine and fourteen was reduced to seven hours; the working day for women workers was fixed at eleven hours and the employment of women and children during night was prohibited. In 1901, for the first time, working hours of male adult workers were fixed at twelve hours per day and the working hours of children reduced to six.

TRANSPORT OF NATIVE LABOURERS ACT 1863

Most of the tea gardens were situated in Assam and by the turn of the century, that is in 1903 there were 479,000 workers permanently employed in the industry besides 93,000 temporary employees. Since Assam was sparsely populated and tea plantations were located on uninhabited hillside, the sorely needed labour had to be imported from Bengal, Bihar and the Chotanagpur areas. The recruitment of labour for tea gardens of Assam was carried on for years mostly by contractors under the provisions of Transport of Native Labourers Act (N.III) of 1863 of Bengal, as amended in 1865, 1870 and 1873. The Act provided for licensed recruitment for transport of workers to the tea gardens. The punishment for refusal to execute a contract at the recruitment depot could extend up to imprisonment for one month and desertion on journey or from the garden up to imprisonment for three months. The harbouring of a deserter could lead to imprisonment for one month or a fine of Rs. 200 or more. It made not only desertion but also indolence on the part of the workers punishable under the 'law'. The planters were given powers to arrest the 'absconders' within the limits of district where they were employed. Breach of contract, a legal jargon/euphemism for refusal to work by a labourer who had taken monetary advance, was liable to criminal action and penalty and a breach of contract during the journey and the place of work was a criminal offence.

Not without reason, the law was condemned as a 'slave law' and a gross violation of the right of personal liberty, turning labour into chattels at the absolute mercy of the planter. There were harrowing tales of enticement, abduction, torture, rape and even murder brought to light by the Indian press at that time. The labour system in Assam was that of indenture by which the labourers went to Assam. Once they had reached the tea gardens they were at the complete mercy of the planters. T. Releigh, law member, speaking on the *Assam Labour and Emigration Bill of 1901* candidly put it thus:

> The labour contract authorized by the Bill is a transaction, by which, to put it rather bluntly, a man is often committed to Assam, before he knows what he is doing and is thereafter held to his promise for four years with a threat of arrest and imprisonment if he fails to perform it. Conditions like these have no place in the ordinary law of Master and Servant. We made them part of the law of British India at and for the benefit of the planters of Assam. The fact remains that the motive power in this legislation is the interest of the planter, not the interest of coolie.[12]

In the late nineteenth century India, the British government, the law givers at that time, were modifying the ordinary law of master and servant in two different and contrary directions at the same time. While in the factories of Bombay and Calcutta, there was an attempt to bring about a certain amelioration in the conditions of child labour and working hours of women and labour of the adult male workers, in the plantation, the clock was being turned back and farm labour was being turned into 'slaves' for a fixed period in the name of freedom of contract.

The manufacturing industry like the cotton textiles, became more 'moralized' by the enactment of factory legislation, to use the phraseology of Engels, not because the British law givers had become more conscientious but because they thought that the extraordinary long working hours of Bombay textiles, gave the Indian industrialists an edge over their British counterparts in Manchester and elsewhere in England.

The Earl of Shaftsbury, speaking in the House of Lord's in 1845 on the need for factory legislation in India and the real motivation behind it, had this to say:

> We must bear in mind that India has the raw material and cheap labour and if we allow the manufacturers there to work their operatives 16 to 18 hours and put them under no restrictions, we are giving them very unfair advantage over the manufacturers of our country and we might be undersold in Manchester itself by manufactured goods from the East.[13]

It would appear anomalous but reflected the peculiarity of the situation that on 22 March 1884, it were the British Textile workers of Lancashire who were demonstrating in front of the office of the Secretary of State for India demanding introduction of factory legislation in India. In 1890, the second Factory Commission was appointed and in 1891, the second factory legislation based on its recommendation was enacted.

But the tea plantations were exclusively owned by the British interest and there was no danger that the sweated slave labour, over whom the planters had almost the rights of life and death would produce any goods cheaper than the one produced in the home country.

This contradiction in their respective attitudes was equally visible on the side of Indian industrialists and their spokesmen. Bipan Chandra in his study *The Rise and Growth of Economic Nationalism in India* recalls that the eventual enactment of Factories Act 1881 was greeted by an uproar of disapproval by the Indian Press. The *Marhatta* at that time edited by no less a person than Bal Gangadhar Tilak, lodged a strong protest against the Act in its issue of 13 March 1881. Among the arguments advanced to show the needlessness of any legislation was the complete absence of any complaint or demand for protection on the part of the workers themselves, who were, it was stated, willing to work for long hours quite voluntarily! *Amrita Bazar*

Patrika of 12 November 1880 wrote: 'If great *zoolam* is practiced upon them, why do they not seek employment elsewhere? Why are they afraid of being dismissed?' But the worst consequence of the Factories Act, according to some critiques would be to sharply swell the number of juvenile criminal offenders, because the boys thrown out of employment will often be forced to beg, borrow or steal. One newspaper remarked that by this legislation, restricting the employment of children—'healthy boys and girls will not be permitted to help their disabled parents'.

There were only rare instances when an Indian newspaper could say:

It is in the nature of masters to try to get as much work out of their servants or employees as possible. The poor servants too are liable to be carried away by their desire to gain money to work themselves to death. Hence the necessity for State interference.

When it came to the Assam Plantation Labour and Emigration Act, the Indian Press and the nationalist leadership reacted sharply. The acute distressing plight of the Assam coolies and the government's attempts to give legal sanction to the system of indentured labour was bitterly criticized and the abuses thoroughly exposed.

When the Inland Emigration Bill was introduced in 1881, and enacted in 1882, it was passionately condemned by the Indian Press for enslaving the coolie and was constantly and vehemently assaulted by the national leadership. It became almost a national demand that all penal laws in respect of emigration and recruitment of plantation labour should be replaced and free emigration of labour introduced in its place.

Bipan Chandra Pal, the famous nationalist leader, in a speech in 1901 brought into focus the question of plantation labour as a part of the larger problem of relations between the working class and the capitalist class.

The question, Mr. Chairman, is an old question—the world-wide question of conflict of labour and capital. The forces of capital already strong in the strength of the all mighty dollar and combining themselves not only to keep out the coolies out of their due reward but also shield even those who are condemned by the Courts and punished by High Court. And when that is done, should not the force of labour also combine? You represent the force of labour. Prince or peasants, Mr. Chairman, we all stand in the position of labourers in this country, and they stand in the position of capitalist.[14]

The pro-labour sympathies of Indian national leadership were, however, roused in the case of plantation labour primarily because of the foreign composition of the capital involved in the tea plantation industry, and did not extend to the labourers working in the Indian-owned enterprises. This was dramatically exposed, when exactly after two weeks of the passing of Assam Labour and Emigration Rule 1901, the Indian Mines Bill came up for discussion and enactment in the legislative council.

The entire Indian Press and all the Indian members of the council opposed the very moderate provisions of the Bill designed for the protection of women and children working in the mines. The Indian National Congress advised the government in 1900 to omit the provisions of Indian Mines Bill so far as they impose restrictions on the employment of labour and on the other hand called for an increase in the wages of Assam coolies.[15]

A cynical illustration of this contradictory attitude was provided by *The Hindu* which wrote in its editorial in March 1903 that a law similar to Assam Plantation Labour Act should be enacted for all employers of labour who experience difficulty not only in gathering labourers but in compelling them to perform their contract. It went on to say:

There need be no class legislation even in regard to Indian coolies, who if they can be made slaves to European planters, may not improperly be made slaves to Indian agriculturists. The Indian coolies are not made to slave for one class only.[16]

While one could well understand, though not condone the opposition of the Indian Press and the nationalist leadership to the passing of the Factories Act, its opposition to the passing of the mild and moderate Mines Act 1901 was not so easily understandable. The clause in the Bill of 1899 prohibiting children between four to ten years being taken underground was attacked on the ground that it would strike at traditional family ties. That no interference from the government was called for because workers concerned had themselves not expressed any desire for such a legislation. The excuse was again trotted out that the measure was intended to help the British coal industry and/or to injure Indian-owned coal mines. It may, however be remembered that at this time, there were very few Indian-owned mines and there was no question of competition between the Indian and British coal industry.

As has been noted above, the coal extracting industry in India at that time employed about 90,000 workers and women and children were employed on an extensive scale in the underground mines. The working conditions of coal miners were extremely pitiable and hazardous, besides being insanitary and stifling. The Act of 1901 itself was an extremely mild piece of legislation providing for inspection of mines, and regulation of employment of women and children underground in a very half-hearted fashion. It is a little known fact that in the coal mines of Bihar and Bengal a system of indentured labour continued till some times after the Second World War on a wide scale, known as Gorakhpuri Labour Camps.

During all these years of industrial legislation in the nineteenth century India, and even in the early decades of the twentieth century, there was no organized Trade Union Movement in the country. The Indian nationalist leaders were blind to miseries that were being produced in the train of industrialization by the factory system of production. They saw behind every move for factory legislation either the hand of Manchester or the fear of competition. The objective needs and interests of the rising working class were not any part of the consideration of the leadership of the national movement at that stage. It is true that Manchester did play a part in its 'moral attitude' because of the fear it had of Indian goods produced with cheap Indian labour working for long hours competing in England itself. One should not however, forget that even in the absence of the organized trade union movement and an effective all-Indian organization giving voice to the demands and requirements of workers, there were many spontaneous strike actions by the industrial workers and on their behalf, which were no less instrumental in bringing some beneficial changes in the field of industrial legislation. V.V. Giri writes:

The founder of the organized labour movement in India may be said to be N.M. Lokhande who was himself a factory worker. In 1884, he organized an agitation and called for a conference of workers in Bombay to make representation to the Factory Commission just then appointed. Lokhande convened a mass meeting in 1890 attended by about 10,000 workers. The meeting adopted a resolution for presentation of a memorial containing demands for limiting the hours of work, provisions for weekly rest days, midday recess and compensation for injuries sustained during work. Lokhande organized the Bombay Mill Hands Association of which he was elected the president. The first working class newspaper the *Dinbandhu* (friend of the poor) was also started by him.

NOTES

1. Prem Sagar Gupta, *A Short History of All India Trade Unions Congress*, p. 3.
2. Cited by Dharni Goswami; p. 14, *Trade Unions Movement in India*, P.P.H. New Delhi.
3. Sumet Sarkar, *The Swadeshi Movement in Bengal*, p. 246.
4. (1870-71) Mad. H.C. REP (XXIV).
5. Second Report on Indian Penal Code to The House of Common; 68 (1848).
6. Maynes Commentaries on Indian Penal Code 382-3 (1878).
7. *Empress vs. Bhagwan Bhisan* (VIII) I.L.R. Bombay 379 (1883).
8. (1865) Mad. H.C. REP 427.

9. (III) I.L.R. ALL 744 (1881) (Supra) Note 4 at 380.
10. (XI) I.L.R. ALL 263 (1889).
11. (XI) I.L.R. ALL 262 (1889).
12. *The Rise and Growth of Economic Nationalism in India*, p. 361. Citing ICP, 1901, vol. XI, p. 133.
13. Cited at p. 7; *A Short History of All India Trade Unions Congress*, Prem Sagar Gupta.
14. *Marhatta*, 1 July 1988 cited by Bipan Chandra at p. 35.
15. Rep.(INC) 1901, p. 168 cited by Bipan Chandra, *The Rise and Growth of Economic Nationalism in India*, p. 398.
16. Bipan Chandra, *The Rise and Growth of Economic Nationalism in India*, p. 328.

3 LABOUR LAWS BEFORE THE FIRST WORLD WAR

From the end of the nineteenth century till sometimes after the First World War, no major industrial legislation was enacted. Except for the Factories Act 1907 and 1911 and the Mines Act 1901, there were no other attempts to regulate the working conditions or ameliorate the plight of the industrial working class. The number of maximum hours in the mines were not fixed and only in the mines considered dangerous to health and safety was the employment of children under the age of twelve or of women prohibited.

It is a truism to say that where legal justice is not available, the demand for social justice nevertheless asserts itself by other means. In case of industrial relations, it is often by means of that expression of collective strength of the industrial working class well known as strike actions. Between 1882 to 1890, the provinces of Bombay and Madras (now Chennai) alone recorded twenty-five strikes. At that stage, there were temporary upheavals, disappearing on some gains being achieved.

However, two strike actions in the period prior to First World War stand out in the annals of this developing struggle for their wider significance as well as an indication of a new trend of militancy and resistance which clearly showed the emerging trade union organization and struggles as part of the national renaissance and resistance and not merely as an 'economic struggle' in the narrow sense of the term. One was the railway strike originating at Asansol in November 1907 and spreading from Allahabad to Tundla. So complete and effective was this strike that the then capital of the British Government in India, Calcutta, was completely cut off from the rest of the country. This strike, which lasted for ten days, was almost immediately followed by the strike of railway engine drivers, firemen, brakemen, etc. in the month of December of the same year. Both were dealt with a heavy hand. Six hundred railway workers were dismissed. British troops were called out and engaged to run the railway and worker assemblies broken up by police and military firing.

The 43-point charter of demand of the railway workers included the demand for the revision of system of fines and penalties which every month substantially reduced the pay packet of the workers on various pretext. It was widely felt that the very system of fines and penalties was introduced in order to find any pretext for the slashing of wages. Other demands included substitution of prevailing time system of payment for the railway running staff with the mile system of payment and improvement of working conditions.

The Statesman of Calcutta noted the significance of these strike actions in the following words:

> There are some factors of the strike of East India Railways, which appear to us to portend great trouble in the future and which the railway authorities will probably feel, on further reflection, worthy of the most careful consideration. An industrial India is rapidly going up and its development will doubtless be attended by the characterization of an industrial community; the formation of trade unions with that concomitant of labour disputes and strikes.

Sometimes later, *The Statesman* again wrote in its editorial:

> No nation, however pliant or submissive, can be flouted to defy it without avenging itself on its oppressors. Unless we are much mistaken, the retribution has made its appearance in Bengal in the form of a consciousness of unity and a realization of the power of combination, the first fruits of which we have just seen in the temporary paralysis of the traffic of the railway in India.

In this context, a note in passing may be made of the mass actions against intolerably long working hours, which were not confined to the major strike actions referred to in the preceding

paragraphs. Ironically enough, the *swadeshi* loom in the
indigenous textile industry and the introduction of electricity
had both contributed to a further lengthening of the working
day despite all the factory legislation on paper. The dawn to
dusk rule was harsh enough and only darkness would give the
hapless industrial worker a respite from backbreaking toil. In
1905, with the introduction of electricity in a number of Bombay
mills, coinciding with a boom in China and home markets (the
latter partly a product of the boycott movement) the working
hours were extended to fourteen or even fifteen hours. Before
reluctant and sometimes half-hearted attempts were made to put
restriction and limitations on this extraordinary exploitation,
massive strikes in Calcutta jute mills and Bombay textiles and
riots demanding a twelve hour day had to precede to give the
'law' the necessary sanction. Not without reason has it been
said that the force behind industrial law is the collective force
of industrial workers to bargain, 'that the mediate and ultimate
source of all industrial law is the fear of collective action by the
workers, their power to collectively bargain reinforced of course
by the power of the State'. (Industrial jurisprudence-Tripathi).
The echo of the railway strike of 1907 and its demand for the
abolition of the system of fines and penalties was to be heard
for quite some time till the Payment of Wages Act 1934 put a
statutory bar on the quantum of fines which could be imposed
on the workers which were not to exceed two paisas in a rupee
of his wages.

The second major strike of the period, that of Bombay
workers in 1908 in protest against the arrest and conviction of
Bal Gangadhar Tilak for sedition, was directly political in
character. Tilak was arrested in Bombay on 26 June 1908 and
the entire city burst out in angry protest as he was put on trial
for sedition. Thousands of people waiting outside the Court
where the trial was taking place clashed with the police force.
In July, Bombay mill workers struck work and came out on the
street in processions. The strike reached new heights when
65,000 of Bombay workers struck work on 19 July 1908. Office
workers joined them on the succeeding days with small

tradesmen, shopkeepers and dock labour. Firing, killing and arrest of striking workers continued but it did not deter the first ever-political general strike on 23 July 1908 in protest against the conviction of Tilak on 22 July. At least 200 people lost their lives in the protest demonstrations. Many more were injured and thousands taken into custody. To the same category belongs the general *hartal* and strike by Muslim and Sikh arsenal and railway engineering workers of Rawalpindi in May 1908. This was part of the nationalist upsurge joined in by the rising industrial working class, which was directly linked with the protest against the deportation of nationalist leaders.

The political general strike of Bombay workers thus heralded the entry of a new social element—the industrial working class in the battle for political independence from alien rule. Its significance as a historical event was noted and hailed by Lenin in the course of his revolutionary writings. The action was also symptomatic of the frustration, anger and deep resentment at the appalling conditions in which the industrial workers had to work in Bombay and other industrial centres. The Textile Factory Labour Committee or the Ferere Smith Committee as it was known, had been set up on 11 December 1906 to investigate the conditions of labour in textile factories. The report of this Committee presented in June 1907 only confirmed the well-known facts of the harsh exploitation of the Indian workers, especially referring to the appalling housing conditions and proposed that factory working hours should be limited to twelve hours a day or seventy-two hours a week.

It might appear small mercy today but in 1911, the factory legislation which was enacted at last limited the working hours of the male workers in the factories to twelve hours a day. No less significant is the historical testimony to the decisive factors behind industrial legislation, i.e., the power of unity, collective strength and organization backed by inevitably innumerable sacrifices, without which not even the most exploitative characteristics of a colonial-cum-capitalist economic system could be even partially curbed.

4 BEGINNINGS OF MODERN INDUSTRIAL LEGISLATION FOLLOWING THE FIRST WORLD WAR

During the war period, both the wave of strike actions and the nationalist upsurge subsided and came to a temporary halt, partly because of the loyalist approach adopted by nationalist leaders including Gandhi towards the war efforts and partly as a result of the repressive and emergency measures adopted by the government of India. The indigenous industries however, witnessed an unprecedented boom precisely during this period. Output of textiles swelled by nearly one-third between the war years of 1914-15 and 1917-18. The number of looms grew from 104 thousand to 116 thousand and the number of workers grew from 2 million 600 thousands to a little more than 2 million 800 thousands. The Tata Iron and Steel Company, the first Indian steel plant, set up in 1908, started working at full capacity to meet the war requirements precisely during this period. The war-time profit enabled the Company to build up two other hydro-power stations. Three cement factories were commissioned where the State purchased most of the products. Production of some chemical goods was also initiated.

For the common people and the industrial working class, the war years, however, meant a sharp increase in their impoverishment due to inflation and spiraling rise in prices, nowhere compensated by any rise in wages or remuneration to the workers. It was therefore no wonder that the end of the First World War saw a big resurgence of strike actions which had been kept in check so long by extraordinary draconian security measures taken during the war.

An indication of the intensity and extent of strike action on the immediate post-war years of the First World War can be

had from the following figures of the number of workers
involved in strike actions:

> November 4 to December 21 1919, woolen mills, Kanpur, 17,000
> men out; December 7 1919 to January 19 1920, railway workers
> Jamalpur 16,000 men out; January 9 to 18 1920, jute mills Calcutta,
> 35,000 men out; January 2 to February 3 1920 general strike
> Bombay 200,000 men out; January 20 to 31 1920 mill workers
> Rangoon 20,000 men out; January 31 1920, British India Navigation
> Company Bombay 10,000 men out; January 26 to February 16
> 1920, mill workers Sholapur 16,000 men out; February 24 to March
> 29 1920, Tata Iron and Steel workers, 40,000 men out; March 20 to
> 26 1920, mill workers Madras 17000 men out; May 1920, mill
> workers Ahmed Abad about 20,000 men out. (R.K. Das, *The Labour
> Movement in India.*)

The cost of living in 1919 was estimated to have risen by 75
per cent to 100 per cent even by conservative estimates over the
level of 1914. The rise in wages which could be secured by
these actions was not more than 35 per cent to 40 per cent and
sometimes even less. Even then, it has been said that the rise in
wages secured in this period was greater than the total achieved
during the previous thirty years. Besides securing certain
increases in wages and remunerations, these strike actions were
also able to secure a ten-hour working day by a further
amendment of Factories Act 1922.

This phase of the widespread and massive actions of the
industrial working class also gave rise to a central organization
of trade unions named the All India Trade Union Congress. At
the top it was led by well-known nationalist leaders like Tilak,
Lala Lajpat Rai, C.F. Andrews, etc. But at the bottom it was the
strike wave of 1920, the consequence of First World War, and
not the least the Russian Revolution which provided the basis
for the setting up of the first countrywide trade union
organization of the workers. Its birth was closely linked with
the post-war national upsurge as well as the upsurge of strike
actions. Lala Lajpat Rai, who was the President of the Indian
National Congress, presided over it. Joseph Baptista the

Chairman of the Reception Committee said in his flowery language: 'The chief business of the Congress would be to sow the seed which like the protesting Amstrad will germinate and grow into a mighty tree of the federation of labour in India which we all desire.' One of the pioneers of the Indian Trade Union Movement, B.P. Wadia had said, 'It is very necessary to recognise the labour movement as an integral part of the national movement. The latter will not succeed in the right direction of democracy if the Indian working class are not enabled to organise their forces and come into their own.'

The moving spirit behind the formation of All India Trade Union Congress and the Trade Union Movement was summed up in these moving words from the first manifesto of the All India Trade Union Congress:

Workers of India! The time has come for you to assert your right as arbiters of your country's destiny. You cannot stand aloof from the stream of national life. You cannot refuse to face the events that are making history today for India. You are the mass of the population. Every movement on the political chessboard, every step in the financial or economical arrangement of your country effects you more then it effects any other class. You must become conscious of you responsibilities. You must understand your rights. You must prepare yourselves to realize your destiny.

Workers of India! Your lot is a hard one. How will you better it? Look at the slaves of the Assam tea plantations, now become desperate. Their real daily wages are less than three annas a day prescribed under government Acts. They are often the victims of brutal treatment working under the lash for unlimited hours, while some of these plantations pay 20 to 40 per cent dividends. They are death and starvation dividends and it is you, your wives, your children who are the innocent, unoffending victims.

Workers of India! The earth is your common heritage. It is not specially reserved for professional politicians or the Simla bureaucrats, or the mill-owing plutocrats. When your nation's leaders ask for *Swaraj* you must not let them leave you out of the reckoning. Political freedom to you is of no worth without economic freedom. You cannot therefore afford to neglect the movement for national freedom. You are part and parcel of that movement. You will neglect it only at the peril of your liberty.

Workers of India! There is only one thing for you to do. You must realise your unity. You must solidify your organizations. Do not look for salvation to the Factories Act. The law cannot give you unity. The law cannot create in you the spirit of brotherhood. That must be your own work. Spoilation of the worker is the cry of the capitalists in field and factory. Let unity and brotherhood of man be your watch-words. Your salvation lies in the strength of your organizations; cling fast to them. Cast all weakness from you and you will surely tread the path to power and freedom.

In the years between 1920 and 1927, there was a certain decline in the number of strikes as well as the number of workers involved in these strikes. But some of the strikes were both powerful and prolonged. The general strike of Bombay workers in 1924 took place as a result of the decision of the mill-owners not to pay bonus on account of allegedly bad trade. The total number of operatives affected were more than 150,000 and the number of work days lost was close upon a million. In 1925 there was a big strike in Jamshedpur and in 1926 May Day was celebrated for the first time in India. In 1928 there were again big general strikes of Bombay textile workers which lasted from April to October. In fact the year 1928, was a year of intense industrial unrest. The number of industrial disputes in the year was 203 as against 128 in 1926, and 129 in 1927, the number of workers involved was 506,851 as against 186,811, and 131,655 of the two earlier years. The number of man days lost rose to the closed figure of 31,647,404 the highest figure on record, till then. In 1929 there was another general strike of Bombay workers against the reduction of 20 per cent in their Dearness Allowance.

This entire wave of 1928 and 1929 was the direct result of the employers trying to pass on the burden of the incoming crisis of depression on to the workers. There were large-scale retrenchment and wage cuts.

To break the resistance of the workers, the British struck a blow early in 1929. On 22 March a number of trade union leaders mainly Communist, were simultaneously arrested all over the country and arraigned in what was known as the Meerut Conspiracy Case. But true to its colonial policy of stick and the carrot, the then India government introduced two pieces of industrial legislation at about the same time, namely, the Trade Unions Act 1926 and the Trade Disputes Act 1929, the two main pillars of industrial legislation, being the parent legislations on the subject, which have provided much of the basis for subsequent legislation in the same sphere in the post-independence period both in Pakistan and India.

The Trade Unions Act 1926 was not merely a procedural and machinery enactment, providing for optional registration of a trade union, carrying the advantage of immunity from civil liability for organizing strikes of the workers. It gave the trade unions protection from the effect of the judgement of Madras High Court in the case of Buckingham and Carnatic Mills, which restrained the Madras Labour Union from interfering with the business of the mills. The decision had resulted in the breaking up of the unions and brought to light the consequences of the absence of freedom of association for the workers. The workers were exposed to criminal proceedings and punishment for any concerted action and officers of trade unions were liable to civil actions for damages for infringing contractual rights and obligations. The Indian Trade Unions Act 1926 gave trade unions legal status and immunity to its officers and members from civil and criminal liability. However, as early as the Delhi session of All India Trade Union Congress, 12, 13 March 1927, the Trade Unions Act 1926 was criticized for its several defects and, it was demanded that:

- The application of the law of conspiracy should be re- moved even in respect of unregistered trade unions, and joint action by workers even without the formation and registration of trade union should be allowed.
- The immunity from civil liability of members and officers should be extended to unregistered trade union.

- The immunity of trade union funds from attachment should be extended to all trade unions.
- The restriction placed upon the powers of the union in spending their funds in helping the working class should be removed.

However under the Indian Trade Unions Act 1926 the registration of the unions was not made compulsory for the purpose of raising of an industrial dispute. Even otherwise the law of conspiracy and civil liability under the Law of Torts did not become operative for any practical purpose.

The subsequent amendments to the Trade Unions Act 1926 in the post-independence period in Pakistan during the first martial law regime in 1958-68 and in 1972 are the subject of discussion in subsequent chapters, belonging to a different historical period.

As noticed earlier, both the Trade Unions Act 1926 and the Trade Disputes Act 1929 were enacted when the second wave of strikes and mass actions by the industrial workers was once again rising in the post-First World War period in consequence of a world-wide economic recession.

A brief summary of the main provisions of Trade Disputes Act 1929 would be worthwhile to understand the legislative intent and the political purposes behind it.

- Prohibition of strike in public utility services, without minimum of fourteen days notice and beyond the maximum period of one month.
- Prohibition of general strikes, sympathetic strikes and/or political strikes altogether, intended to compel the government to take a particular course of action.
- Strike for industrial disputes outside the industry was similarly prohibited.
- Reference by the government of any existing apprehended industrial dispute to a conciliation board or a court of enquiry.
- Compulsory reference of an industrial dispute to conciliation board or court of enquiry where both the parties representing

the majority or each of them make an application to that effect.

However, neither the report of the court of enquiry nor that of the conciliation board were in any way binding upon the employers or the workers and were not enforceable in the Court of Law, so that the prohibition of a strike by government did not mean that the industrial dispute would be adjudicated upon.

This Act was criticized in the 9th session of All India Trade Union Congress at Jharia by its President M. Daud in the following words:

The introduction of Trade Disputes Bill in the last session of the Indian Legislative Assembly clearly gives a clue to the attitude of the government towards the movement. The Trade Disputes Bill is reactionary in character. If this were passed into law than practically all trade unions would be dwarfed in their development. The trade unionist and other philanthropic workers would be punished in effect in cases of pressing the legitimate claims of the working class when occasions need such action. Strikes, the last recourse of urging the demand of the workers would be declared illegal in case the employers are not given sufficient time to recruit men in place of strikers. Organisers of strike would be punished in some industries and strikes would be illegal. By these legal provisions, the government practically intends to stifle all sorts of labour movement that are felt necessary to safeguard its interest. If this reactionary law finds place in the statute, the trade union movement, instead of developing, would be gradually eradicated to the best bargain of capital. The government is bent upon suppressing the movement by the reactionary black law.

The statement of the objectives and reasons of the first Indian Trade Disputes Bill, stated:

The outbreak of industrial unrest on a large scale was a feature of the period succeeding the close of war and led the government of India to explore the possibility of providing some machinery for the settlement of industrial dispute. The inquiries made for this purpose in 1920 led to the conclusion that in the conditions then existing, legislation for this purpose was not likely to be effective.

The succeeding years saw a distinct change in the position by reason of the growth of organization of industrial workers and of the increasing influence exercised by public opinion on the course of disputes. And in 1924, the Government of India prepared a draft bill for enabling the investigation and settlement of trade disputes and circulated it in order to ascertain the views of those directly interested and of the public generally as the subject.

As a result of enquiries made in 1924-25 and the experience which has become available since that period, the Government of India is satisfied that legislation for the prevention and settlement of trade disputes is likely to prove of considerable value and the present bill has been prepared for this purpose. (Statement of objects by the Government of India.)

Commenting on the Trade Disputes Act 1929, the Royal Commission of Labour in India observed (report page 338):

The measure which passed into law in 1929 does not provide for any standing industrial court. Disputes can be referred to court of enquiry or reconciliation, which are appointed to enquire and to report into specific matters referred to them, consist of one or more independent persons. Board of conciliation consists of an independent chairman and ordinarily of other members who may be either independent or may represent parties to the dispute. It is their duty to endeavour to investigate the dispute, primarily with a view to settlement and secondly with a view to enlighten the public regarding its merits.

The Act also contains provision rendering punishable by fine or imprisonment lightning strikes or lock-out in certain public utility services and embodies provisions aimed at the prevention of general strikes; the latter provisions are based on the clauses of British Trade Disputes and Trade Unions Act 1924. The

Commission observed regarding the future legislation on the subject:

> We do not doubt that some statutory machinery will be permanently required to deal with trade disputes and it will be necessary to consider the form which such machinery should take before the Act expires in the first half of 1934.

The Act was made into a permanent measure in 1934.

FACTORIES ACT 1922

The ILO Conventions ratified by the British India Government necessitated the amendment in the Factories Act of 1922 fixing the maximum working hours for adults (Male and Female) at eleven hours a day or sixty hours a week with half hour rest for more than five hours continuous working and a weekly holiday. The employment of children below the age of twelve was completely prohibited, and the working hours of children between the ages of twelve and fifteen were restricted to six hours work a day with half hour rest interval and a weekly holiday with an additional requirement of a physical fitness certificate. The definition of a factory was extended to those employing twenty persons or more. Some of the provisions of the Act could be made applicable by the provincial government to other manufacturing concerns having ten or more workers. The principle of overtime wages was introduced for the first time, at one and quarter time the normal wages for work beyond sixty hours a week. The standard for ventilation and artificial humidity were improved to prevent health hazards of the workers. Certain minor amendments were made in 1923 and 1926 to restrict double employment of children and through an amendment in 1931, the provincial government was empowered to make rules for providing precaution against fire inside the factories. The Factories Act 1922 was drastically amended in 1934, and the enactment was promulgated in the light of the recommendations of the Royal Commission of Labour. This enactment incorporated detailed provisions for health and safety and the inspection was made more effective. The new Factories Act 1934 was amended from time to time until the time of partition. Therefore, it will be quite appropriate to deal with this Act 1934 in the next chapter.

MINES ACT 1923

The Mines Act 1901 had neither fixed the maximum working hours for adults nor protected the conditions of work for women and children. Its provisions were quite inadequate and its administration unsatisfactory due to overlapping functions of the central and the local governments. This new Act redefined 'mine' to include any excavation irrespective of depth for search or the obtaining of minerals. It prohibited the employment of children under thirteen years under the ground. It prescribed a fifty-four hours a week for underground and sixty hours a week for above the ground for all male adults, and under certain conditions, it authorized the government to restrict the employment of women below the ground. Rules and regulations were framed in respect of health and safety that prescribed safety conditions for the mining operations. Inspectorate, Mining Board, Committee and Court of Inquiry were established and the manager of the mines was made responsible to keep adequate supply of drinking water, maintain satisfactory arrangements, sanitary conditions and if notified, to keep medical supplies, first aid appliance, stretchers and medicines handy. It also required the extract of the Law to be displayed at the mines and penalty of a fine of Rs. 500 for infringement of any provision was retained as before.

MERCHANT SHIPPING ACT 1923

This Act was not essentially a part of labour legislation as it was enacted to consolidate various marine laws. Only chapter II of the Act dealt with the recruitment, service conditions and welfare of the marine labour. This was amended in 1931 to give effect to ILO Convention 15 and 16 whereby the minimum age and medical fitness of young persons at sea was prescribed. Under Convention no. 22 of ILO, the Article of Agreement between the shipmaster and the persons employed for sea service were prescribed. According to the original Act and the amendment in 1931, the seamen were enabled to enforce the agreement entered at the time of engagement. The shipping master was also required to enter in the voyage book the details of work done by seamen and to settle their dues before discharge and to pay his fare through to the country of origin if discharged at a place other than the place he was engaged. Employment of a person under the age of fourteen in any capacity and under the age of eighteen as trimmer and stockier was prohibited except under certain specified conditions. No person below the age of eighteen was to be employed or carried on the sea to work in any capacity unless he was declared physically fit by the prescribed medical authority and a certificate to that effect obtained. Provisions for accommodation, catering of the crews and medical attendance while at sea and aboard the ships were also prescribed. A minimum of 72 cubic feet accommodation was prescribed for each crew member with sufficient drinking water while at sea.

THE WORKMEN'S COMPENSATION ACT 1923

Prior to the Workmen's Compensation Act, there was no prescribed/settled law to the claim of workmen for compensation for injuries, disablement or death arising out of and in the course of employment. Only the Fatal Accident Act 1885 could be invoked, but the procedure was cumbersome and expensive. Section 43-A of the Factories Act empowered the criminal courts to order the whole or part of the fine imposed for offences causing work injury or death to be paid as compensation to an injured worker or to his legal heir in case of his death, which was quite ineffective and hardly provided any relief. The Workmen's Compensation Act could be considered as a forerunner of future social security legislation. The Government of India had appointed a committee in June 1922 to suggest measures for such an enactment which formed the basis for the law prescribing compensation in respect of unemployment due to work injuries not resulting in permanent/partial disability and injuries resulting in death. Separate compensation was prescribed for each of these categories in the schedule to the Act, which was revised from time to time.

Initially and until 1947, the Act was applicable to workers drawing a maximum of Rs. 300 per month and employed in factories, mines, ports, railways, tramways, telephone, and telegraph, etc. According to an estimate, about nine million workers were provided cover under this enactment. In order to avoid delay and procedural complexities, the government was empowered to appoint Compensation Commissioner vested with powers of a Civil Judge for expeditious disposal of the claims of the injured workers under this enactment. In order to implement ILO conventions pertaining to occupational diseases, an amendment was incorporated in 1926 whereby any worker who was incapacitated for work due to occupational diseases was also to be compensated as if he was incapacitated due to work injury.

5 GREAT DEPRESSION AND THE ROYAL COMMISSION ON LABOUR

The unprecedented economic depression of 1929-30 led to a drastic worsening of the conditions of the Indian working class. Thousands of workers in every industry were retrenched. Forty thousand workers were sacked in the Indian Railway alone in 1931. Inevitably, there were also prolonged and embittered strikes. The following figures show the number of strikes during 1930 to 1937.

Year	No. of strikes and lockouts	No. of work-people involved	No. of working days lost
1921	396	600,351	6,984,426
1922	278	433,434	3,972,727
1923	213	301,044	5,051,704
1924	133	312,462	8,730,918
1925	134	270,423	12,578,129
1926	128	186,811	1,097,478
1927	129	131,655	2,019,970
1928	203	506,851	31,647,404
1929	141	532,016	12,165,691
1930	148	196,301	2,261,731
1931	166	203,008	2,408,123
1932	118	128,099	1,922,437
1933	146	164,938	2,168,961
1934	159	220,808	4,775,559
1935	145	114,217	973,457
1936	157	169,029	2,358,062
1937	379	647,801	8,982,000

Source: R. Palme Dutt, *India Today*, pp. 410-11.

It may be recalled that the complete independence resolution had been adopted as the political goal of the country in the 1929 session of the All India Congress Committee at Lahore and 26 January 1930 was observed as the First Independence Day throughout the country. While Gandhiji was preparing for his *Salt Satyagraha*, there was a wave of strikes throughout the country including powerful mass demonstration, the Meerut Conspiracy Case against trade union/communist leaders, the Chittagong armoury raids cases, the refusal of Gharhiwali solders to open fire at the people in Peshawar led by Chandra Sing Gharwal and the virtual taking over by the people of the Peshawar administration for ten days. The year 1934 saw yet another wave of strikes directed against the rationalization scheme of the big employers, wage cuts, retrenchments, etc. Sixty-one thousand workers were thrown out of employment in Bombay alone, wage cuts ranged from 7 per cent to 45 per cent. In Ahmedabad, wage cuts ranged from 12 per cent to 25 per cent, and in Madras 15 per cent. Consequently, a general strike took place in Bombay from April to June and in Sholapur from February to May. As many as 159 strikes took place in 1934 involving 220,808 workers and 4,755,539 man days lost.

It was in this background that the British government announced the appointment of a Royal Commission on Labour, the Whitley Commission, to enquire into the conditions of industrial labour in India and make appropriate recommendations. This Royal Commission on Labour was the foundation stone of the labour policy of the British government in subsequent years.

While the majority in the All India Trade Union Congress strongly moved for the boycott of the Whitley Commission, as the national movement did in the subsequent years in respect of the Simon Commission set up for the so-called constitutional reforms, a small number of liberal trade union leaders like N.M. Joshi, V.V. Giri, S.G. Joshi and W.V.R Naidu made it a point to split the trade union session. Incidentally, this session at Nagpur on the question of boycott of the Whitley Commission was presided over by Jawaharlal Nehru in 1929.

The resolution of the All India Trade Union Congress on the appointment of the Royal Commission on Labour stated:

a. Whereas the Whitley Commission has been appointed by the British imperialist government ostensibly to inquire into the conditions of labour;

b. And whereas the Government's open and brutal attack upon the Trade Union Movement by means of repressive legislation and the wholesale arrests of the trade union leaders and the wholesale raiding of the trade union offices and the suppression of strikes with the help of the police and military shows clearly that the government does not intend to allow the workers to develop their organizations to obtain better conditions;

c. And whereas the masses of India cannot agree to the *bona fides* of the government to set up such a Commission and consider it only a camouflage to hoodwink the workers and facilitate their exploitation by suppressing the growth of militant trade unions;

d. Therefore, this Congress is of the opinion that this imperialist Commission should be completely boycotted by all sections of the exploited masses of this country, generally and by all the trade unions and other working class organizations particularly and that demonstrations and meetings should be organized to protest against the imposition of such a Commission at every place where the Commission goes.

The recommendations of the Royal Commission of Labour when they were published in 1935 were a mixed package. Mr Jamna Das Mehta stated at the second session of National Trade Union Federation at Nagpur in 1935 that 'Of the 457 total recommendations, 24 were considered unnecessary, no action was taken in 68 cases, 65 were implemented and 8 recommendations were under legislation. About the rest, it was difficult to say what was going to happen.'

The following labour laws were enacted or amended by the central government of British India in subsequent years mainly on the basis of the recommendations of the Whitley report:

- Workmen's Compensation (amendment) Act 1933, extending the Act of 1923 to cover railways, tramways, mines, seamen, docks, persons employed in construction, operations relating to telephone, telegraph, overhead electric lines, electricity and gas generating stations, etc.
- Children (pledging of Labour) Act 1933, prohibiting the pledging of labour of children under 15 years age by their guardian.
- Factories Act 1934 superseding all earlier Factories Act, laying down a ten hours day and 54 hours week for duty in non-seasonal factories. For seasonal factories 11 hours a day and 60 hours a week.
- Dock Labour Act, 1935.
- Mines (amendment) Act, 1935.
- Payment of Wages Act, 1936.
- Employers Liabilities Act, 1938.
- Motor Vehicles Act, 1939 (only Section 65 relating to working hours of transport workers).

6 PROVINCIAL AUTONOMY UNDER 1935 ACT AND THE LABOUR LAWS

By 1937, significant changes had taken place in the political landscape of the country with the implementation of provincial autonomy and the induction of popular ministries at the provincial level. People expected a new deal and there were a wide range of expectations. There was a wave of enthusiasm for organizing trade unions and developing trade union struggles. The AITUC called upon the Congress ministries to implement its own election manifesto and asked the labour legislators to support the Congress members in the implementation of their programme. Both the number of organized trade unions and their membership rapidly increased. During the three years, 1937, 1938 and 1939, the number of registered trade unions went up from 271 to 430, to 562 and their membership from over 260,000 to about 400,000.

Soon the organized industrial working class and the Congress ministries came into conflict. The year 1937 unleashed yet another big wave of strikes. Sharp conflict arose in relation to the question of trade union rights, trade union recognition, right of strike, the right to hold meetings, picketing, etc.

The strike waves which started in 1937, grew to newer heights in 1938 and a total of 399 strikes involving 401,075 workers took place covering a loss of 9,198,708 man-days. There was general strike of Kanpur mills in May and June 1938 when about 50,000 workers struck work, as a protest against the rejection by the Employer's Association of the recommendations of an enquiry committee. In Bengal, the enactment of a Jute Ordinance resulted in cutting down the already low wages of the workers by about 16 per cent; 25,000 jute workers were involved in a prolonged strike. The Trade Disputes (amendment)

Act was passed in 1938 in this background and the statement of objectives and reasons of the bill stated:

> The Trade Disputes Act was passed in 1929, originally for a period of five years and was converted into a permanent measure in 1934. It was reviewed by the Royal Commission of Labour and was criticised in certain minor respects by two courts of enquiries appointed under it. The proposals contained in the Bill represent the changes which, in the light of experience gained of its working and opinion expressed upon it, appear to be desirable.

The amending act altered the definition of an illegal strike, included within the list of utility services any inland stream vessel and tramway service which government might notify and any undertaking which supplies power to the public and extended the definition of 'trade dispute' to include any dispute and difference between employers and employers also.

However, the most important and practical amendment was a provision for the appointment of Conciliation Officers with certain powers though the Provincial Governments were left with the discretion to make such an appointment. The work of conciliation officers included not merely, like the Courts of Enquiry and Boards of Conciliation, the 'investigation' and settlement of disputes but they were charged with the duty of 'preventing disputes'.

The trade dispute legislation during this period was attended to with some closer attention by the Provincial Governments rather than by the Centre for obvious reasons because provincial governments were popularly elected government within the framework of the 1935 India Act and were more concerned with the sovereign powers in the province. In 1934, the Trade Disputes Conciliation Act was passed in Bombay. This was before the popularly elected governments had taken over in the provinces. However, this Act only provided for the appointment of a Labour Officer to look after the interest of the workers in cotton mills and to represent their grievances with a view to getting them redressed. There was also a provision for the appointment of a Commissioner of Labour to act as an ex-officio Chief Conciliator in cases where a Labour Officer did not succeed. It has been claimed for the Bombay Trade Disputes Conciliation Act 1934 that it had succeeded in practically eliminating industrial strikes in textile mills in Bombay city. However, the period of three years was too short a period to make any assessment in this respect. With the inauguration of the provincial autonomy there was a resurgence of labour trouble in Bombay as well as in other textile centres. This recurrence of labour trouble arose out of high expectation and was attributed to hopes raised among the workers with the coming into power of popular ministries. The workers naturally thought that with the popular ministries in power their grievances could be more readily redressed. Thus installation of the popular ministries acted as a spur to a new wave of strikes and industrial actions on the part of the workers, ushering a new industrial and labour legislative policy at least on a provincial level. Among them special mention may be made of:

BOMBAY INDUSTRIAL DISPUTES ACT 1938

This Act could really be called the precursor of Industrial Disputes Act 1947. The main feature of the Bombay Industrial Disputes Act 1938 passed by a Congress ministry was to make it obligatory for the unions, the workers as well as the employers to resort to the machinery of conciliation and arbitration and to exhaust this machinery before resorting to a strike or lock-out. The Act also provided for the first time for the recognition of the unions by the employers concerned, subject to the unions fulfilling certain requirements as regard membership.

Strikes and lock-out were made illegal until the whole of the machinery for discussion and negotiations provided for by the Act had been made use of. The right to declare a strike or a lock-out could be exercised only within a period of two months after the failure of the conciliation proceedings. Conciliation would start to function as soon as a dispute appeared likely to occur. Probably the most important provision of the Act was that an employer or workman who desired to make a change in wages or hours of work or other conditions of employment was required to give a notice of his intention to do so to the prescribed authorities and no change could be affected until the machinery of the Act had functioned to the fullest extent. This provision still forms an important ingredient of the Industrial Disputes Act 1947 in India.

RECOGNIZED UNIONS

The concept of 'recognized unions' was also introduced for the first time under this enactment. Where recognized unions existed, the conduct of negotiations was a matter between the employers and the recognized unions. Where there were no recognized unions, 'directly elected representatives' of the workers or a Labour Officer conducted the preliminary discussions. If an agreement was reached during the discussions, they were to be registered. However, if the parties failed to reach an agreement, a trade dispute which was only considered as 'likely to arise', till that stage, was now considered to have occurred and the official conciliator was to step in and endeavour to bring about a settlement of the dispute. In case of failure of conciliation or if the government so decided, a Board of Conciliation could then be appointed. Where employers and the union agreed to refer the dispute to arbitration, the official machinery was not to be brought into operation in the earlier stages and could or could not operate in the later stages. The Act also provided for the setting up of an Industrial Court presided over by a High Court judge or a lawyer qualified to be a High Court judge. This Court was to act as a tribunal for voluntary arbitration on matters submitted to it by the parties to a dispute. It also functioned as a court of final appeal in numerous cases arising out of the working of the Act. The Court was to decide whether or not a strike or lock-out was illegal and questions of interpretation of agreements and awards would also come before it.

The Bombay Trade Disputes Bill 1938 was criticized by the All India Trade Union Congress as uncalled for, reactionary, retrogressive, prejudicial and harmful to the interest of the workers, making unnecessary discrimination and distinction between different kind of unions (the recognized and unrecognized unions), 'calculated to create slave unions' working under the direction and control of the employers. The Bill was further criticized as putting unnecessary restrictions on free, proper and healthy development of unions working on real trade union lines. The All India Trade Union Congress expressed its regrets that the Bill not only 'repudiates the Congress election manifesto but even ignores the progressive recommendation of the Royal Commission on Labour.' 22 January 1939 was observed as an all-India day of protest against the Bombay Industrial Disputes Act 1938.

A memorandum submitted by N.M. Joshi, the liberal trade union leader to the National Planning Committee set up by the Indian National Congress contained the following observations:

> The human agents of production as the industrial workers are called, should have a voice in deciding upon the conditions of work under which industry should be run. Industrial strikes and class wars are likely to be accentuated in systems in which labour conditions are determined according to the rigid law of supply and demand. Mitigation of these evil is to some extent possible if the working class is allowed or enabled to have its say in all matters concerning the industry, especially matters regarding conditions of work and wages.

This was probably the first attempt to project trade union rights and working-class demands as part of struggle for human rights. Its realization was, however, still a long way to come in a world torn between global wars.

7 SECOND WORLD WAR AND PRE-INDEPENDENCE INDUSTRIAL LEGISLATION

The Second World War broke out in September 1939. On 2 October 1939, one of the biggest political strikes of Bombay working class took place when 90,000 Bombay workers put down their tools in protest against the Second World War. The declaration of war immediately led to a steep rise in the cost of living and profiteering of all sorts. Strikes for increased wages and dearness allowance followed all over the country. There were general strikes in Bombay and Kanpur. On 5 March 1940, 1,200,000 workers of Bombay struck work lasting for sixty days. On 10 March, 350,000 workers went on a strike. The Kanpur strike involved 30,000 workers and lasted for ten days, 20,000 Calcutta seamen went on strike at the end of March 1940.

In the background of the country-wide strike wave against the economic effects of the Second World War, a new series of industrial enactments came into being. The Bombay Industrial Disputes Act 1938 was amended in 1941 and under Section 49-A of the Act, the Provincial Government was authorized to refer any industrial dispute to the Arbitration of the Industrial Court, if it was satisfied that the industry concerned was likely to be seriously affected and the prospect and scope of employment curtailed as a result of continuance of industrial dispute, or a serious or prolonged hardship to a large section of the community was likely to be caused or a serious outbreak of disorder or breach of public peace was likely. The Industrial Disputes Amendment Act 1941 also specified that any strike or lock-out taking place before the completion of this arbitration proceeding was illegal.

ESSENTIAL SERVICES ACT 1941

In the same year that is 1941, another law known as the Essential Services Maintenance Ordinance was enacted, according to which no person engaged in any employment declared as essential services could leave the area of employment declared as essential services. Any refusal by any worker engaged in such employment to obey 'reasonable order' given in the course of the employment, or habitual absence from duty or absconding were made offences liable to severe penalties. The employer, who discharged any person engaged in the employment without 'reasonable cause' or discontinued or closed down his works or caused its discontinuance, was also guilty under this Ordinance and subject to its penal provisions. The law which was essentially a war time emergency measure of the Second World War has continued to remain on the Statute book both in India and Pakistan till the present times being enacted in Pakistan as Essential Services Act 1952 and extended every six months in some of the selected/or notified industries like oil, petroleum, etc. Its continuous extension over a number of years has deprived the affected workers of the right of collective bargaining. The right to approach the Labour Court against unlawful dismissals to seek the relief of reinstatement was also taken away in Pakistan by the Supreme Court in PLD 1981 SC 13 on an interpretation of these provisions which was thankfully restored—years later by another decision of the Supreme Court reported as 1989 SCMR 1549. A special authority, the National Industrial Relations Commission was authorized to determine the terms and conditions of service in notified industries in Pakistan subject to the approval of the Federal Government.

DEFENCE OF INDIA RULES (RULE 56-A)

In April 1943 Rule 56-A was added to the Defence of India Rules, which prohibited '*hartals*' in certain classes of employment. The term '*hartal*' was defined as any concerted cessation of work by a body of persons in any place of employment, which was not a stoppage or refusal in furtherance of a 'trade dispute' with which such a body or persons were immediately concerned. This provision was specifically meant to cover cases of political general strikes or sympathetic solidarity strikes on the part of the workers.

DEFENCE OF INDIA RULES (RULE 81-A)

In these series of war time emergency trade legislations put on the statute book, special reference should be made to rule 81-A of the Defence of India Rules, which was enforced in January 1942. The provisions of this rule may be summarized since they were reflected in principle on a more permanent basis in the Industrial Disputes Act 1947.

The Central Government got the authority under this Rule to prohibit a strike or a lock-out in connection with any trade dispute and to require employer, workmen or both to maintain such terms and conditions of employment which may be determined in accordance with the order, refer any trade dispute for any conciliation or adjudication, enforce the order or any decision of the authority to whom a trade dispute has been referred for adjudication and for other accidental supplementary matters.

The Bombay Industrial Relations Act 1946 continued the emergency industrial legislation adopted during the war period, removing some of the defects of the earlier legislation and incorporating the amendments made in 1941. The chief features of the new Act were 'Statutory machinery of compulsory conciliation and compulsory arbitration with the awards made binding on the parties.' All disputes that were not referred to arbitration were to be settled by the compulsory conciliation, which were to be completed within three months. The State Government could make it applicable to the industries or the area within which Bombay Industrial Act 1938 was not applicable by notification in this behalf. The State Government was also empowered to refer to the arbitration of Labour Courts having ordinary and special jurisdiction in local areas for which they were constituted. These courts were authorized to decide industrial disputes referred to them for arbitration, to decide the legality or otherwise of a strike, lock-out or changes in Standing Order, and were empowered to enforce their decisions in the matter. The Labour Courts thus became Courts of Arbitration and Industrial Courts the Court of Appeal.

The industrial legislation from the Trade Disputes Act 1929 to the enactment of Trade Disputes Act 1947 have been summarized in the following words:

> Experience of the working of the Trade Disputes Act 1929 has revealed that its main defect was that while restraints had been imposed on the rights of strikes and lock-out in public utility services, no provision was made to render the proceedings instituted under the Act for a settlement of an industrial dispute either by reference to the award of conciliators or to a court of enquiry conclusive and binding on the parties to the dispute. This defect was overcome during the war by empowering under rule 81-A of Defence of India the Central Government to refer the industrial disputes to adjudicators and to enforce their award. Rule 81-A which is to lapse on 1st October 1946 is being kept in force by the Emergency Power (continuance) Ordinance, 1946 for a further period of 6 months, and as industrial unrest, in checking which this rule has been so useful, is gaining momentum due to the stress of post-war readjustment, the need of permanent legislation in replacement of this rule is self-evident. This Bill (the Industrial Disputes Bill) embodies the essential principles of Rule 81-A, which has proved generally acceptable and keeps intact for the most part the provision of Trade Disputes Act 1929.

The two institutions, for the prevention and settlement of industrial disputes provided for in the Bill, were the Works Committee consisting of one or more members, and an Industrial Tribunal composed of members possessing qualification ordinarily required for appointment of judges of the High Court. Powers were given to the appropriate government to require

Works Committee to be constituted in industrial establishment employing one hundred or more and their duties were to remove causes of frictions between employers and workmen in day to day working.

INDUSTRIAL DISPUTES ACT 1947—CONTINUATION AND CHANGE

The Industrial Disputes Act 1947 was the last piece of labour legislation prior to independence and partition of the sub-continent. This Act, although with some very substantial amendments in certain spheres, continues to govern industrial relations in India. In Pakistan, it was repealed and substituted by Industrial Disputes Ordinance 1959, which in turn gave way to a short-lived Industrial Disputes Act 1968 and ultimately the Industrial Relations Ordinance 1969. The latter, in the course of last seventeen years has undergone many substantial amendments. Yet the main outlines of the parent legislation can still be discerned in the features of the second or third generation of Pakistan labour legislation in the field.

INDUSTRIAL DISPUTES

The preamble of the Industrial Disputes Act 1947 described the purpose of the Act to be 'investigation' and 'settlement' of industrial disputes, which was defined as a 'dispute between workmen and employers, workmen and workmen, employers and employers connected with the terms and conditions of employment of any person including the question of employment or non-employment or the terms of employment or conditions of labour of any person.' Reference to dispute between workman and workman or between employers and employers has come to be, with passage of time more than an anachronism particularly after IRO when an industrial dispute is deemed to arise only if raised in the prescribed manner either by the CBA or the employer. The provision remains on the statute book adding to the very considerable confusion, which is the hallmark of the Act. The Industrial Disputes Act 1947, claimed to regulate the trial of strength between capital and labour expressed in the form of 'strike' and 'lock-out'. It has been described as a piece of legislation for a smoother process of 'collective bargaining' between the 'buyer' and 'seller' in the labour market. As stated by Paul Davis and Mark Freedland in their work *Labour Law*, the public policy in England (UK) since the First World War was to encourage collective bargaining as a method whereby employers and workers organized into trade unions, could determine for themselves the rules that should govern the employment relationship. The consequent autonomy to the employers and the unions and the decentralization of power that it implies were long-standing and valued features of English industrial relations system.

The study of industrial law in England is usually the study of use of law to promote the spread of collective bargaining as a substitute for unilateral managerial prerogative. Much the same thing could not be said about industrial relations law in India or Pakistan. Here the emphasis was on regulating the 'strikes' and 'lock-out'. Indeed in the South Asian sub-continent 'collective bargaining' and 'trade unions' have come to be looked upon with a very considerable amount of suspicion, as almost a variety of 'subversive activities'. The 'autonomies' and 'decentralization of power' in the matter of regulating employer relationship claimed in the case of UK was very seriously restricted in the case of the sub-continent. The talk of 'strike' and 'lock-out' as two sides of the same shield was also somewhat misleading since, 'lock-out' rarely if ever became a necessity on the part of the employer to 'bargain' with the workers since he had more effective prerogatives available like 'retrenchment', 'closure' and layoffs to lay down its own terms of employment in a labour surplus market.

In the industries which were termed 'Public Utility Services' the Act regulated 'strikes' and 'lock-outs', by making it compulsory to give a fourteen days' notice by the workers or the employers, as the case may be. This notice would then set in motion the obligatory conciliation machinery under the law but if the conciliation efforts failed, it was left to the option and discretion of the government to refer the dispute to industrial adjudication or let the parties decide the issues by a trial of their 'collective strength'.

The schedule of public utility concerns originally attached to the Industrial Disputes Act 1947 has been very much extended in the subsequent years, both in India and Pakistan, so that compulsory strike/lock-out notice and obligatory conciliation effects have now become the rule rather than an exception in most of the industries.

In Industries, other than those falling in the category of public utility concerns, there was no compulsory requirement of a prior notice of strike/lock-out. However, in these industries, if there was an existing settlement, strikes and lock-outs were prohibited on 'matters covered by the settlement' and in such case the prohibition was complete during the subsistence of the settlement but on matters not covered by it, the parties were free to have a fresh trial of strength.

Reference of an industrial dispute in non-public utility services was entirely discretionary with the appropriate government and the exercise of this discretion has been held by the courts in India, to be entirely within the 'discretion' of the government and not subject to judicial review or control. It has been repeatedly held by the superior courts in India that even where the government had formed an opinion that an industrial dispute exists or is apprehended it would still be free to consider whether it should be expedient to refer the dispute. The only obligation imposed upon the government in case the government chooses not to make the reference is to record the reason for the same and to communicate it to the concerned parties. The government was sole arbiter of the factum of existence of industrial dispute and it was its sole discretion to decide whether it would be expedient to make a reference or not. In public utility service, the general rule (by the use of the word 'shall' instead of 'may') was for reference of dispute to adjudication.

The exception to it was provided in the circumstances when the government came to the conclusion that it was not in the 'public interest' to do so or that the dispute was 'vexatious' or 'frivolous'. Very wide discretionary powers indeed are thus vested in the government under the Industrial Disputes Act 1947 even in respect to reference of an industrial dispute to adjudication. As a necessary corollary to this differentiation between public utility concerns and non-public utility concerns, conciliation proceedings were compulsory in the former and optional in the later.

Apart from the government making a reference of an existing or even 'apprehended' dispute to an industrial tribunal or conciliation board, the only other way for such a reference, was for both the parties to the dispute to make jointly or separately an application for such a reference. Even in such a case, the government reserved the right to refuse such a reference on the ground that either of the parties did not represent the majority of the disputant party. Quite obviously it could have reference in the majority of cases only to workers' side.

Reference of the industrial dispute to adjudication was therefore optional with the appropriate government, since the making of the reference was discretionary with the government and there was no other way for the invocation of the adjudication machinery. This appeared to provide a greater scope for collective bargaining only where a strike or lock-out was not of much consequence.

Industrial adjudication under the Industrial Disputes Act 1947 was to be resorted to not as a rule but as an exception. Apparently it allowed for a greater freedom of action both on the part of the employers and the workers. In actual practice, the provisions of law operated to restrict the option available to the side represented by the workers.

It may be recalled that all strikes, whether in the public utility concerns or any other industry were also prohibited during any period in which a settlement or award was in operation in respect of a matter covered by the settlement or award.

Since, for the purpose of a valid settlement, it was not necessary that it should be arrived at between the parties, representing the majority on each side (as was the requirement for a reference of a dispute in adjudication) and since a settlement between a union and the management became binding on all workers whether they belonged to the union or not, the employers could easily avoid a strike by means of a settlement arrived at with a 'pocket union.'

It could therefore be said that the freedom of industrial action on the part of the workers was more illusory than real. Even then, this situation could be favourably compared with that prevailing in the later periods, in Pakistan between 1959-69 when 'compulsory adjudication' completely replaced collective bargaining.

Gradually, over the years, the principles of industrial adjudication have evolved for which a comprehensive machinery had been set up under the Industrial Disputes Act 47, which was substantially different from the concept involved in the adjudication of civil disputes. A very important element of industrial adjudication came to be recognized as 'social justice', equity and good conscience.

In the case of *Labour Relations Board of Saskatchewan vs. John East Iron Works Ltd.* the Privy Council observed as follows:

The jurisdiction of the Board (Labour Relations Board) is not invoked by the employees for the enforcement of contractual rights. Those whatever they may be, can assert elsewhere. But his reinstatement, which the terms of the contract of employment might not by themselves justify, is the means by which labour practices regarded as unfair are frustrated and the policy of collective bargaining as a road to industrial peace is secured. It is in the light of this new conception of industrial relations that the questions to be determined by the Board must be viewed. (AIR 1949 PC 129).

Legislation regulating the relations between Capital and Labour has two objects in view. It seeks to ensure to the workmen who have not the capacity to treat with capital on equal terms, fair return for their labour. It also seeks to prevent disputes between employer and employee so that production might not be adversely affected and the larger interests of society might not suffer (AIR 1957 SC 38).

The principles underlying industrial adjudication have also been recognized by the Supreme Court of Pakistan in PLD 1961 SC in the words that, 'the task of Industrial Court in adjudication and determining industrial disputes is not to discover what the right of the parties are, under the existing contract of service, or even under an existing law. It really extends to the making of a new contract, limited only by the general principles of whether it is in keeping with equity and good conscience.'

INDIVIDUAL DISPUTE AND INDUSTRIAL DISPUTE

Under the Industrial Disputes Act 1947, the raising of an industrial dispute was not an exclusive right of even a registered trade union, much less a recognized union or a collective bargaining agent. It was held that even a written demand or its rejection was not a prerequisite of the existence of an industrial dispute. But distinction was clearly drawn between an individual dispute and an industrial dispute. However aggrieved an individual workman might be against his termination or dismissal, he could not invoke the machinery of industrial adjudication, unless his cause was taken up by a substantial number of workers which transformed an individual dispute into an industrial dispute. But the story did not end here, because even in cases where industrial dispute was taken up by a substantial number of workmen, the reference of the dispute to adjudication remained within the discretion of the Provincial Government. The discretion whether to refer the dispute to adjudication or not could not be subject to judicial review or interference by the court of law. Thus, in cases where the government refused to refer a dispute to adjudication, the only alternative left open to the workers was to resort to strike action.

By an amendment of Industrial Disputes Act 1947 (India) in 1965, Section 2-a provided that any dispute between an individual workman who has been discharged, dismissed retrenched or otherwise terminated and his employer, connected with or arising out of such discharge, dismissal etc. would be deemed to be an industrial dispute, notwithstanding that no other workman or union is a party to the dispute. But the adjudication of such an industrial dispute still remained subject to the discretionary powers of the government to make a reference.

PART 2

LABOUR LAWS
AFTER
INDEPENDENCE
IN
INDIA AND PAKISTAN

8 Labour Legislation after Independence

Pakistan inherited the labour laws of pre-partition India, just as it did the administrative system, civil and criminal laws and pre-independence constitution, the 1935 India Act.

However, Pakistan hardly inherited any industry; which constituted only 9 per cent of the industrial establishment of pre-partition India. The areas constituting Pakistan were more pre-dominantly agricultural with a highly entrenched feudal system than what was left behind in India. The Trade Union movement in Pakistan was extremely weak and confined to one or two big cities and could not be said to have had any place in the national politics which had brought about the creation and birth of the new State.

The numerical weakness of industrial workers in Pakistan could be also gathered from the fact that in 1949, factories employing twenty or more persons and using mechanical power, to which the Factories Act applied, employed a total of less than 200,000 (181,752) workers. Mines employed less than 10,000 (9413) workers, railway less than 150,000 (135,000), dock labour numbered 15,000 and another 16,000 were employed in shops and establishments. Sea-going vessels were estimated to be employing about 125,000 workers. Industrial workers were thus estimated to be near about 480,000 an infinitely small part of the total population of the country which was about 75 million in both the wings, a mere 63 persons per 10,000 of population. The workers employed in agriculture are however not taken into account. They were and continue to be outside the pale of any labour legislation in Pakistan. Similar was the condition of plantations, cottage industries, inland water transport and small commercial establishments whose total number of workers far exceeded the number of workers employed in organized industries.

THE FIRST TEN YEARS OF INDEPENDENCE

Till the promulgation of the first Martial Law and the induction of the full-fledged martial law regime under Ayub Khan in 1958, legislation in the industrial field in Pakistan followed the lines laid down by the British rulers in the last decade of their rule in the subcontinent. But, even during the decade before the promulgation of Martial Law in Pakistan, the trade union movement and its organization was not looked upon with any great favour by the administration in the newly created State. As stated earlier, Pakistan had inherited only 9 per cent of the industrial establishments existing in the subcontinent at the time of independence. Though there were a number of old and strong trade unions organization in Karachi, as in the Cement Industry, Karachi Electric Supply Corporation and the Karachi Port Trust, the level of organization of industrial workers was considerably lower than in India as was the existing level of industrial development in this country. The requirement of rapid industrial development was universally looked upon as a question of life and death for the new nation with a far greater acuteness than in neighbouring India. It was therefore not difficult for the leaders of the government to put forth the idea and get it more or less accepted in the country that the demands of industrial workers for social justice or more equitable share in the fruits of their labour could wait till such time the country became stronger and a basis for rapid industrial development was laid down. Similar policy postures were also adopted in the presentation of its labour policy by the government of India, where also it came to be emphasized again and again that question of distributive justice did not arise for as long as the country did not have enough to distribute.

The first Prime Minister of Pakistan, in his address to the first Tripartite Labour Conference said:

We must create conditions which are favourable to labour. My government will take all necessary steps to see that labour gets its due share in all enterprises... Labour must remember that the interest and welfare of Pakistan come before the interest of an individual or class of individuals and must not do anything, which in any way weakens Pakistan. If Pakistan endures and prospers the problems that labour faces can be solved.

This policy was more clearly spelled out in the 1955 statement of labour policy by the Government of Pakistan.

In this country where industrialization is in its early stages, government is anxious that while labour should get its just rights, industry should not be hampered by unnecessary upheavals and strikes. Government therefore believes in promoting the settlements of disputes between employer and employees in the interest of industrial peace through constitutional means.

The Industrial Disputes Act 1947 was amended by Act XXVII of 1948 and further amended by Act XIV of 1956, whereby 'any undertaking, establishment or installation relating to defence services were included in Public Utility Service', compulsorily requiring fourteen days notice before proceeding on strike/lock-out. Other industries contained in the annexure to the Development of Industries Act 1949 were included in the same category by the latter amendment. Employment of Children (Amendment) Act 1951 prohibited employment of children under fifteen years of age in the transfer of passengers, goods or mail by railway or connected with the handling of goods within the limit of any port. Young persons between the age of fourteen to fifteen were prohibited from doing night work on the railways and ports. Similarly, an amendment in the Mines Act 1923 prohibited night work by women and children employed in the mines. Both these amendments followed ILO Convention 89 and 90.

Pakistan Essential Services Act 1952, resurrected the wartime legislation of the British government namely Essential Services Act 1941, making it a penal offence for any employee in the notified industry to absent himself or abstain from employment either singly or in concerted action with others. The termination of service of the employee without reasonable excuse was also made an offence but did not provide any protection to the workers. The law enforceable initially for six months could be extended in its application indefinitely after every six months.

Towards the close of the first decade of independence, in India, as in Pakistan, the public euphoria of subordinating the interest of the most down-trodden sections to the greater interest of the nation (relegating 'social justice' to 'requirement of development'), was coming to an end. Industrial unrest was growing because of increasing economic hardships with no end visible to the growing economic crisis. In Pakistan, industrial unrest was compounded with political conflict and confusion at the top and what may be termed as a general weakness of the political process and democratic awareness at the grassroot level.

Through 1956-58, the days lost through work stoppages in Pakistan dramatically increased and in 1957-58 a total of 517,000 man-days were lost, which was the highest figure to date in the country. The strike of the Adamjee Jute Mills workers and those of Chanderguna Paper Mills were high water marks of the militancy of the industrial working class in East Pakistan which got inextricably combined with the general political upsurge in that part of the country. In the Adamjee Jute Mills strike, and the riots that followed, it was estimated that about 300 persons and a smaller number at Chanderguna Paper Mills were killed. These militant actions of the East Pakistan working class and the brutal repression let loose against it became the immediate excuse for dismissing the popular ministry of the Jukta Front in East Pakistan elected in the first ever general elections in Pakistan trouncing the Muslim League. How these events became precursors of much wider changes and ultimately of the alienation and separation of East Pakistan are matters relating to a different study. Here it may suffice to say that the working class unrest and its growing militancy, both in East and West Pakistan was probably one of the important factors which led the administration to the conclusion that it could not continue to govern this country with the help of the democratic institutions which the founding fathers had fought for in both the countries in the movement of independence namely a democratically elected parliamentary system. The martial law or semi-martial law regimes which came into being from 1957 in Pakistan set up their own legal framework including a new framework of labour laws corresponding more closely to the requirement of the private sector in the country.

9 FIRST MARTIAL LAW IN PAKISTAN AND THE INDUSTRIAL DISPUTES ORDINANCE 1959

The Industrial Disputes Ordinance 1959 enacted by the first martial law regime, followed the structural pattern of the Industrial Disputes Act 1947 but fundamentally changed the underlying policy of the legislation and also curtailed drastically the rights in respect of collective bargaining and the formation of trade unions.

The distinguishing feature of the 1959 Ordinance was that strike and lock-outs in public utility services were completely prohibited though this was done in a rather devious manner. A strike or lock-out as under the 1947 Industrial Disputes Act was prohibited without giving a strike notice and before the expiry of the notice period, which was made obligatory in public utility concerns. It was also prohibited during the conciliation proceedings, which were to commence on the serving of the notice of strike. Under the 1947 Industrial Disputes Act, when no settlement was arrived at during the conciliation proceedings and the appropriate government made no reference adjudication of the industrial dispute, a strike could be resorted to even in the public utility concern. What was new under the 1959 Industrial Disputes Ordinance was that the strike or lock-out was also prohibited before making an application for adjudication of the industrial dispute before the industrial court. Adjudication therefore became compulsory in public utility concerns and resort to strike or lock-outs were completely prohibited. Prohibition of strikes or lock-outs during the pendancy of an industrial dispute before an industrial court followed as a matter of course. Finally, as before strike/lock-outs were prohibited on matters covered by a settlement or award of the industrial court. Thus a strike/lock-out practically came to be prohibited at all stages and a notice of strike or lock-out was required to be served only to invoke the jurisdiction of industrial court. The appropriate government where it was itself a party to an industrial dispute could declare the dispute to be frivolous or vexatious whereafter the matter could not be taken up with an industrial court for adjudication. The distinction between public utility service and the non-public utility service was also considerably whittled down. This was done first by expanding the definition and scope of the 'public utility concern' under the 1959 Ordinance which now included almost all the existing industries in Pakistan in the schedule one of the Act which listed industries of public utility type. The holding of conciliation proceedings was made obligatory in non-public utility concern also whenever an industrial dispute was deemed to exist or was apprehended where after all the prohibitory clauses in respect of strike/lock-out became applicable to non-public utility concerns. The policy underlying the Industrial Disputes Ordinance 1959 could thus be appropriately described as a policy of compulsory adjudication with an almost total ban on strikes and lock-outs in the public as well as non-public utility concerns.

As a necessary corollary to the purpose of introducing compulsory adjudication, the law now enabled the party to whom a failure certificate had been issued to make an application to a labour court for the adjudication and determination of the industrial dispute.

It is interesting to note that by 1961, that is two years after the 1959 Ordinance, the martial law regime felt it necessary to restrict even the scope of industrial adjudication and make it more difficult for the workers to approach the industrial court. By way of amendment of the Industrial Ordinance XVI of 1961, the industrial court was required:

Before proceeding with the adjudication and determination of the industrial dispute in respect of which an application has been made under sub section 5 of section 5, the industrial court may determine in a summary way, the question if raised by any party to the dispute other than the appropriate government that all or any of the matters constituting such dispute is frivolous and vexatious.

The words 'frivolous' and 'vexatious' were kept too vague to give a wide scope for the use of discretion by the industrial courts and its misuse by the employers. These restrictions gave the impression that the main purpose of the Industrial Disputes Ordinance 1959 was to clear the way for 'the unhindered development of free enterprise', that is unhindered either by actions of collective bargaining on part of the workers or by adjudication of industrial disputes by the industrial court. Probably it was apprehended that some elements of 'equity' 'social justice' and 'reasonable standard of living' for the working class were bound to creep in the decision of the industrial courts, which may not be favourable to the climate of 'free enterprise and investment, which was required to be created'.

The main purpose of the Ordinance was in fact achieved by an absolute martial law regime and draconian measures adopted in support of its edicts. Even the formation and functioning of trade unions was put to severe restrictions and curbs. By virtue of Ordinance IV of 1960 and subsequently Ordinance XI of 1961 the Trade Unions Act 1926 was drastically amended to provide for recognition, besides registration of trade unions. Chapter III-A was introduced on the recognition of trade unions. The recognized trade unions had to show a membership of not less than 10 per cent of the total number of workmen employed exceeding the number of the members of every other trade union and became entitled on a memorandum of recognition so signed between an employer to receive and reply letters of and grant interviews to the executive in connection with any such matter.

It was also considered necessary to bring the trade unions under control and to 'save' them from the influence of 'outsiders' and extraneous political influence. For this purpose, the Trade Unions Amendment Ordinance 1961 (Ordinance X of 1961) provided under an amendment to section 22 of the

Ordinance that 'no person shall be elected as an officer of the trade union, who is an outsider but is not a paid whole-timer of the trade union'. Thus a person, who was not an employee of the industry, could become an officer of the trade union only if he was a paid whole-time worker of the union. At the same time a person could not become a paid whole-timer of more than one registered trade union.

Mahbub ul Haq, the eminent economist, summarized the government policies in the following words:

> The commitment to growth philosophy was so wholehearted that all policies were subordinated to it... the government went out of its way to encourage a handful of industrialists, big farmers and capitalists to save and invest. Generous fiscal concessions were available; taxes were light and freely evaded. Policies of economic liberalism were followed without adequate safeguards so that incentives were used for those who already had the basic economic strength to utilize them...Real wages of industrial workers declined by over one third over the last eight years (i.e., 1960 and 1968).

It was thus clear that the adjudication machinery in exercise of the principles of 'social justice', 'equity' and 'good conscience' failed to be effective where the right of strike and the collective bargaining agent was so completely muzzled.

The martial law regime, after more or less completely stifling the trade unions and confining industrial disputes to the Law Courts, thought it necessary to appear to provide some relief to the workers in other fields. Thus the Industrial and Commercial Employment Standing Orders Ordinance 1960 which enacted the Model Standing Orders was promulgated, doing away with the cumbersome process of certifying Standing Orders separately for separate establishments. The Working Journalists Act 1960 made the provisions of Standing Orders Ordinance applicable to journalists and provided for the setting up of Wage Boards to settle the terms and conditions of journalists in the newspaper industry. Provincial Employees Social Security Ordinance 1965 was enacted incorporating provisions of sickness benefits, accident compensation and maternity benefits, etc. but its application was dependent upon government notification. It was not till a later period that it became an effective social security legislation. Companies Profits (Workers Participation) Act 1968 was introduced more or less as a substitute for a statutory provision for profit sharing bonus, becoming payable at a sliding rate on completion of given years of service for different wage groups. These measures could not and did not reverse the trend of continuing fall in real wages, the hallmark of economic liberalism.

10 THE LAW OF TRADE UNIONS AND INDUSTRIAL DISPUTE

The first martial law regime of Ayub Khan, which so ruthlessly suppressed the trade union movement in particular and the democratic aspirations of the people in general, met its nemesis when it began celebrating the 'glorious decade' of its regime in 1968. A massive popular movement spearheaded by students and the industrial working class in both wings of the country overtook the regime and the legal system of labour relations established by it. The Industrial Disputes Ordinance 1968 and West Pakistan Industrial and Commercial Employment Standing Orders Ordinance 1968 were quickly put on the statute book to stem the tide of discontent but barely did so. The former was to be replaced very shortly by a new law and the latter very substantially modified in 1972-3. When President Ayub Khan was forced to resign, he handed over power to another martial law regime headed by Yahya Khan, which was treated as an interim martial law regime. The regime announced a new labour policy, recognizing that in the past labour had not been given a fair deal.

The labour policy statement of 1969 preceding the enactment of the new industrial disputes legislation in Pakistan in 1969 was the handiwork of the second martial law regime in Pakistan under Yahya Khan, a surprisingly 'radical' document, coming as it did as the policy statement of a martial law regime which followed the resignatxion of Ayub Khan. In a sense, the policy statement bore the marks of the pressure of popular movement of the preceding year which had ended in a transitional 'martial law' promising to hold the first ever general elections in the country, a promise which for once was kept. At the same time, the imprint of its authorship of a martial law regime was no less visible in the very large exemptions written into it, which went beyond even the 1959 Industrial Disputes Ordinance.

The policy statement began with an unexpected admission that:

> The government recognizes that the worker had not had a fair deal in the past. In a period of growing prosperity and rapidly increasing production, the worker's real income and living conditions have remained static and in many cases have even deteriorated.

The policy statement recognized the prevalent inefficiency in the Pakistani industry inspite of most well-equipped machines and use of advanced technology and attributed it primarily to the failure of management-worker relationship. It accepted that conflicts were 'inherent in a worker-employer' relationship and noted that a country like Pakistan had a large surplus labour force, and that the industrial worker, a recent immigrant from rural life is unused to the discipline and authority relationship of the industrial environment.

The importance of the trade union movement in Pakistan was also underlined by recognizing that in conditions of 'too many workers chasing too few jobs', it was only through the membership of a trade union that a worker could safeguard his rights and further his interests.

The reasons for the slow growth of the trade unions in Pakistan were also analysed in an entirely new approach, as due to:

1. The attitude of the workers who accepted *landlord-tenant model* of relationship in industrial life.
2. The negative attitude of the employers towards the trade unions.
3. The attitude of the government which had hitherto tried to 'keep production going' by discouraging and prohibiting the expression of industrial conflict.

Measures to encourage the growth of trade unions in Pakistan were spelled out and the new concept of a 'Collective Bargaining Agent' put forth which enjoyed the widest support among the workers through a secret ballot. It categorically rejected the concept of 'recognition' by the employers introduced by section 28/B of Trade Unions Act 1961 under Field Marshal Ayub Khan. It promised reduction of the administration's powers to interfere with the affairs of trade unions to a minimum. However with all its recognition of the need and importance of trade unions, there was a total exclusion of persons employed in installations and services 'connected' with defence forces and those employed in the administration of the State, when the 'policy' came to be legislated. This was a retrograde departure from the earlier laws including the Industrial Disputes Ordinance of 1959 which had included undertakings, establishments or installations relating to Defence Services, Pakistan Printing Corporation, etc. within the definition of the public utility services, which were compulsorily required to serve fourteen days strike notice, whose workmen could form their trade unions and invoke the jurisdiction of industrial courts to adjudicate the industrial dispute raised by the union and the workers. Another interesting feature of the new law was that in non-public utility concerns, a strike could not be prohibited nor the dispute referred for adjudication before the strike had lasted for one month. This provision was subsequently repealed.

The other important aspect of the Policy Statement, was a division of industrial dispute between Matter of Rights and Matter of Interests. Subsequent amendment in the definition of industrial disputes excluded altogether 'enforcement of guaranteed rights' from the definition and scope of an industrial dispute as such. Conflicts of interests were defined as matters which could be determined only through collective bargaining supported by the workers right to strike and the employers rights to lock-out. Matters of Rights were those which could be enforced as a pre-existing right under a law, settlement or award. The word 'right' in this connection meant a right which the workers could claim as having been already so determined/adjudicated upon. In fact adjudication came to be associated with questions of interests or demands and 'enforcement' with questions of rights which already existed, pre-determined and pre-existing either by law or an award or settlement.

The law also introduced the concept and machinery for the determination of a collective bargaining agent which was made more restrictive and exclusive in the next period.

THE LAW OF TRADE UNIONS

The Industrial Relations Ordinance 1969 was substantially modified and amended by the succeeding regime of Zulfikar Ali Bhutto both as a civilian martial law administrator and the Prime Minister of the country. The amendments during the period continued with the restriction of the second martial law regime in applicability. The amendment allowed the party raising an industrial dispute to take the matter for adjudication by the labour court before or after the commencement of the strike. It imposed stiffer conditions for securing the status of a collective bargaining agent and even for the registration of trade unions and provided a machinery for the redress of individual grievance. The law on the formation and registration of trade unions has been amalgamated and consolidated with the law on industrial disputes under the Industrial Relations Ordinance 1969. The registration of a trade union is restricted by the condition that its membership is limited only to workmen actually employed in the establishment or industry concerned though it permits one-fourth of the total number of office-bearers to be from amongst those not so actually employed. A further restriction was imposed in case there already exists two or more registered trade unions in the same establishment, group of establishments or industry. In such a case, the union seeking registration has to show at least 20 per cent of the total number of workmen employed in the establishment as its members. This is justified as a restriction on the multiplicity of trade unions. Considerable powers were conferred upon the Registrar of Trade Unions by making every change in the office-bearers of a registered trade union and/or its constitution subject to its registration with the Registrar. In case there is a dispute about the changes in the office-bearers or the Registrar rejects a change among the office-bearers, the Labour Court, on an application or appeal, may order fresh election of the union under the supervision of the self-same Registrar of Trade Unions. The only right which a registered trade union has under the Pakistani law is in its incorporation as a body corporate, the limitation of the law of conspiracy and immunity from civil suit in certain cases and a right to contest in the ballot for the determination of a Collective Bargaining Agent. A registered trade union in Pakistan does not have any right to raise an industrial dispute, serve any strike notice or represent the workers in any proceedings unless it has been certified as a Collective Bargaining Agent under the process laid down under the law. The law only gives protection to office-bearers of a trade union against dismissal during the pendency of the application for registration. Similar protection is extended to office-bearers of a registered trade union during the pendency of proceedings before a conciliator or a Labour Court or Tribunal.

In the post-independence period, both in India and Pakistan, while lip service is paid to the fundamental right of association and formation of trade unions, their registration and raising of industrial disputes by them is subjected to ever increasing restrictions under various legal provisions. In Pakistan, the list of areas, industries and establishments, where the rights of combination, including the right to form trade unions is totally denied, has gone on increasing under the Industrial Relations Ordinance 1969 promulgated by the second martial law regime and continued during the short periods of succeeding civilian administration. Originally, section 1, sub-section 3 of IRO excluded employment in the armed forces and police, in services and installations connected with or incidental to the armed forces and employment in the administration of the State from the application of the IRO. Subsequently, under the third martial law, the list of exclusion was extended to include:

a. members of the security staff of Pakistan International Airlines Corporation or drawing wages in such group not lower than Group V in the Corporation or as the Federal Government by notification in the special gazette specify,

b. employees of Pakistan Television Corporation or the Pakistan Broadcasting Corporation,

c. employees of the Pakistan Security Printing Corporation or the Security Papers Corporation,

d. employees of an establishment maintained for the treatment or care of the sick, infirm, destitute or mentally unfit persons,

e. a member of watch and ward in the security or fire services of an establishment engaged in the production or transmission or distribution of liquid gas or liquid petroleum gas.

The Labour Policy Statement of 1969, while recognizing that it was only through the membership of a trade union that a worker could safeguard his rights and further his interests, excluded a large segment of workers from the right to form trade unions, which was much larger than under any previous industrial law.

Employment in the administration of State as well as in the services and installations 'connected with' or 'incidental' to the armed forces, were excluded from the trade union law. Even though 'employment in the administration of the State' was narrowly interpreted in some cases by the Superior Courts in Pakistan to mean 'persons employed in connection with the activities in exercise of its sovereign powers, including action of legislative, judicial and executive wings' (1975 PLC 361, PLD 1978 Karachi 503, 1980 PLC 244), there were other cases like (PLD 1991 SC 553) Controller of Stationery and Forms, Government of Pakistan, where it was held that since it supplied printing materials to the various organizations relating to armed forces and also for the requirement of other government departments and other State organizations and functionaries and police, its employees were excluded from the ambit of the Industrial Relations Ordinance 1969.

On the question of what is connected with or incidental to armed forces, a very wide interpretation of the 'Connection' was given in the case of Canteen Stores Department (1983 SCMR 1101) wherein it was held that though the Canteen Stores was a private commercial organization, its employees could not form a trade union since it formed the basis of an efficient canteen organization in peace and war for armed forces anywhere in the country and operational areas during the war. Similarly in the case of United Builders and Associates (PLD 1976 SC 855) where the army were engaged in getting a highway of national importance constructed through the contractors, it was held that the construction was a matter connected with the armed forces and so the right of trade union organization and raising of industrial disputes for increasing their wages was denied to the workers.

Even though railway and postal departments workers were specifically included in the scope of Industrial Relations Ordinance, a notification issued by the government of Pakistan has excluded an overwhelming majority of railway workers from the Industrial Relations Ordinance and the right to form trade unions on the wide plea that since the railway lines are engaged in transportation of troops during peace and war it is 'connected with' the armed forces. The notification covers all the twenty railway lines in the country. 130,000 workers of WAPDA are excluded both from Industrial Relations Law and the Standing Order Ordinance by virtue of Ordinance XX of 1998. Additionally the entire Water and Power Development Authority was handed over to the army in exercise of a constitutional provision where the army could be called in aid of civil power.

Yet another category of workers excluded from the trade union laws are 'civil servants', who may not be employed in the exercise of sovereign powers of the State but only because they are government servants and are neither covered by the Workmen's Compensation Act, nor by the provision of the Factories Act. The Superior Courts have spelled out their exclusion from the trade union and industrial laws from a reading of the constitutional provision (Article 212) and the Services Tribunal Law that the Tribunals (in this case the Provincial or the Federal Services Tribunal) set up by the appropriate government shall have exclusive jurisdiction in matters relating to the terms and conditions of the employment including disciplinary proceedings. The result has been that a *chowkidar* even though 'technically' described a workman, employed in the National Savings Unit, was excluded from the provision of Industrial Relations Ordinance 1969 (PLD 1992 SC 127: *Fakir Muhammad vs. Director National Savings*).

Similar was the fate of *beldar*, fitters, electricians and other manual, skilled and other workers employed in various government departments like the Forest Department or the Agricultural Department unless they were shown to be covered by the Workmen's Compensation Act or the Factories Act when they cease to be civil servants.

The workers employed in the government departments are also excluded on the argument that the government departments do not carry on any 'industry'. It may be borne in mind that the Services Tribunal at the Federal or the Provincial level do not have any jurisdiction to determine fresh terms and conditions of employment like the Industrial Tribunal. Workers who are technically government servants are thus denied their right of forming trade unions and raising industrial disputes.

In Pakistan, an amendment in the Federal Services Tribunal Act 1973, brought on the statute book on 7 June 1997 has declared 'service under any authority, corporation, body or organization established by or under a Federal law, or which is owned or controlled by the Federal government or in which the Federal government has a controlling share' to be service of Pakistan and every person holding a post under such corporation, body or organization is a civil servant for the purpose of Federal Services Tribunals Act 1973. As a consequence of this amendment, the jurisdiction of Labour Courts has also been taken away to decide upon cases of individual grievance of workman against termination in case of nationalized industries, banks or corporation. It appears to leave the question open whether the Services Tribunals have the same extensive jurisdiction in fact and law as the Labour Courts under IRO 1969. It is also a moot question if the Federal Services Tribunal can adjudicate an industrial dispute of these workmen with respect to improvement in terms and conditions of their employment.

The government of Pakistan has also exempted the industries in the export processing zone not only from the law of industrial relations vide Export Processing Zone Authorities Ordinance (IV of 1980), and workers prohibited from forming trade unions in the industries situated in the export processing zones, ostensibly to attract foreign investment. All other labour laws have also been made inapplicable. The 'excluded' workers are estimated to constitute more than 50 per cent of all workers employed in various industrial and commercial establishments in Pakistan who are deprived of their trade union rights directly or indirectly.

Another curtailment on the right of trade unions to elect office-bearers not actually employed in the industry was introduced by section 27-B of the Banking Companies Ordinance which prohibited the trade unions of the banking companies from electing an office-bearer who was not actually employed in the bank. Even a dismissed worker of a bank is excluded from holding any post in the union. A similar provision is suggested in the draft labour policy of the government of Pakistan circulated recently. The Supreme Court of Pakistan has held in PLD 1997 SC 781 that under Article 17(1) of the Constitution of Islamic Republic of Pakistan, the right to form a trade union is a fundamental right which includes the right to act as a collective bargaining agent. But the right to go on strike or go slow are not rights which can be spelled out from section 17(1) of the Constitution. Therefore, the right to form a trade union including a right to act as collective bargaining agent continued to exist but outside the legislation of Industrial Relations Ordinance 1969. This, however, could be excluded in its application to selected categories of workmen even though theoretically they may have the right to form trade unions or claim the status of collective bargaining agent. The anomalous and quite a self-contradictory position taken by the above Supreme Court decision is largely due to the amalgamation of trade union laws and the law of trade disputes in a single piece of legislation under the IRO. The Supreme Court of Pakistan could have consistently held with its views that the right of strike is not a fundamental right with the view that section 5 to 14 of IRO dealing with the registration of a trade union and section 22 dealing with the determination of a collective bargaining agent fell within the scope of fundamental rights and were protected by the constitution. It was anomalous on part of the Supreme Court to hold that collective bargaining is a fundamental right but the right to strike is not, ignoring the fact that collective bargaining necessarily entails rights to withhold labour when the terms of employment are not agreed upon. The right to slow down has never been claimed or recognized as a right of the trade unions or of Collective Bargaining at all, and could not be bracketed with the right to strike. The Supreme Court decision also ignored the existence of Essential Services Act, which was first enacted in 1941 and re-enacted in 1952 taking away the right to strike in essential services without taking away the right to form and function trade unions.

The administration in the Labour Department has been given a big lever to interfere both in the internal elections of the unions as well as the determination of the collective bargaining agent. The changes in the office-bearers of a registered trade union has to be registered with the Registrar of Trade Unions and the same Registrar is given the powers to hold fresh elections of a union in case of a dispute among the union members. With the introduction of a check-off system in favour of CBA, where the membership subscription is deducted at the source from the salaries/wages of the workers, the CBA becomes closely linked up and associated with the employers and even dependent upon them. A proposal by the government of Pakistan in its draft labour policy that those registered trade unions not securing a minimum number of votes in a ballot should be de-registered appears to be a step in an adverse direction. In order to put an end to the unfortunate trend of the institution of collective bargaining agency becoming a corrupting influence in the hands of unscrupulous employers and the bureaucracy, and also to save the trade union leaders from turning into trade union bureaucrats, it may be advisable to allow registered trade unions who have not been elected as CBA, some role to represent their members as in proceedings under section 25-A IRO and even in respect of raising industrial disputes on behalf of their members. The provision under the Industrial Relation Ordinance that no industrial dispute shall be deemed to exist unless raised in the prescribed manner that is by the CBA giving the two stage notice of bilateral negotiations followed by a strike notice requires revision and change. Protection given to the officers of the CBA against arbitrary dismissals, etc. is available only during the pendency of conciliation proceedings or proceedings before a Labour Court/Tribunal. Since bilateral negotiation do not constitute the commencement of any proceedings, no protection is available to the workers for that period and gives the employers an upper hand.

Collective Bargaining Agent

The institution of collective bargaining agent introduced for the first time in Pakistan under the Industrial Relations Ordinance 1969 provided that proceedings for the determination of a collective bargaining agent can be initiated by any registered trade union only if it has more than one-third of total number of workmen employed in the establishment as its members. The employer or the government could initiate the proceedings on their own. Where there is only one registered trade union in an establishment, even then it has to prove before the Registrar Trade Unions that it has one-third of the total number of workers as its members. The Registrar of Trade Unions is authorized to conduct the ballot, declare the results and issue a certificate of collective bargaining agent to the winning union, which however must secure the votes of at least one-third of the total number of workmen employed. Not all the workers employed in the establishment are entitled to vote. The voter in the ballot for the determination of the CBA must be a member of one of the contesting trade unions, must be employed for at least three months in the establishment and his name must be borne on the voters list prepared by the Registrar of Trade Unions. The decision of the Registrar of Trade Unions in the matter of determination of collective bargaining agent is not subject to appeal or revision before any Labour Court, Tribunal or Commission, leaving the process open to many abuses and manipulations.

Since the collective bargaining agent has the exclusive right to represent workmen in any proceedings, enter into any settlement with the employers and raise an industrial dispute, other registered trade unions do not have any function left to perform during the two years that the term of a collective bargaining agent subsists after having been so elected. Any other registered trade union can challenge the existing CBA and call for a fresh ballot only at the end of its two years' term, but the challenging union has to prove that it has at least one-third of the total number of workmen as its members. With no activity or function left, a non-CBA union would be hard put to fulfill this condition.

In India, the laws relating to the registration of trade unions had not undergone any substantial modification since 1926 and even after 1947, except that by virtue of the enactment of Chapter III-A the Registrar of Trade Unions is required to maintain a list of the 'approved trade unions'. The condition of entry in the approved list includes a membership of not less than 15 per cent of the employees employed in the industry in that local area for at least three months; a provision in the constitution of the union for a minimum membership fee and audit of the accounts by government auditors, provision for regular meetings of the executive committee and for a procedure for declaration of strike supported by the majority of members. The rights conferred upon approved unions include the right to collect trade union dues on the premises, use of a notice board on the premises, to hold discussions on the premises with the members of the union, to meet and discuss with the employer or his representative for the removal of grievance of the members.

However, other unions are not debarred from raising industrial disputes or representing workers in proceedings before an industrial tribunal.

Certain provincial amendments in India provide for a reference of any dispute about who is the lawful office-bearer of a registered trade union to the Industrial Court which can be made either by the officer claiming the office or by the Registrar of Trade Unions.

At the end of the century, the trade union rights are subject to severe pressure once again. The policies and legal provisions curtailing these rights as during the first martial law in Pakistan are again on the agenda and sought to be revived. The right of the trade unions to elect a maximum of 25 per cent of their office-bearers from amongst those not actually employed in the industry is dubbed as the failure of the workers to realize the importance of 'internal leadership' and urges upon them not to accept 'outsiders' as their leaders according to the Draft Labour Policy of Nawaz Sharif. The trade unions on the other hand, consider the move as a subterfuge of the employers not to allow those whom they remove from service to remain in the leadership of the unions. In other words, the proposal is seen as a move to control the unions by removing from employment those not found pliable by the employers and then also closing the doors of the union organization upon them. Moreover, as held by the superior courts both in India and Pakistan 'insider' office-bearers are subject to the discipline of the employers even in their function as office-bearers of the unions, seriously curtailing their independence, freedom of action and speech as office-bearers of trade union. A great threat to the trade union and the wage standards of the workers in countries like India and Pakistan also arises from 'casualization of labour' and the massive induction of contract labour, wiping out the gains of labour legislation in the social field, which shall be discussed subsequently.

The right of trade unions to set up or support their own candidates in the Provincial, Federal Assembly or the local bodies and for this purpose set up their voluntary political funds,

which had been surreptitiously removed from the provisions of
IRO 1969 assumes special importance in order to give political
voice to the industrial workers in the affairs of the country and
to safeguard their interests in the legislative field.

INDUSTRIAL DISPUTES LEGISLATION

The definition of the term 'Industrial Dispute' under the Indian
law remains substantially unaltered, where it need not be 'a
conflict of interest' but may also be 'conflict of rights' or 'legal
dispute', concerned with the interpretation of the existing terms
or with their enforcement. The insertion of section 2A in the
Industrial Disputes Act 1947 introduced a deeming clause so
that an individual dispute connected with the discharge,
dismissal, retrenchment or termination was to be deemed to be
an industrial dispute, notwithstanding that no other workman or
no other union espouses the dispute.

In Pakistan, an amendment of Industrial Relation Ordinance
1969 excludes matters of enforcement of rights guaranteed or
secured under the law, settlement or award from the definition
of any industrial dispute and provides a separate machinery for
its enforcement.

A notice of strike or lock-out is required under the Indian
law only in case of public utility services, and such a notice can
be given by a union or the elected representatives of workmen.
No strike notice was required in case of establishment not
connected with public utility. Under the Pakistani law an
industrial dispute can only be raised by a collective bargaining
agent and no industrial dispute shall be deemed to exist unless
raised in the prescribed manner by a collective bargaining agent
or by the employer. Such a strike notice is to be given by
collective bargaining agent in industrial establishments whether
in public utility or not and has to be preceded by a notice of
bilateral negotiations and only in case of failure of bilateral
negotiations, or a lapse of a minimum period, a notice of strike

can be served by the collective bargaining agent or a notice of lock-out by the employer.

Conciliation proceedings both under the Indian and Pakistani law are deemed to commence on the date when a notice of strike or lockout is received by the conciliation officer or under the Indian law on the date of the order referring the dispute to a Conciliation Board.

However, under the Indian law, commencement of conciliation proceedings and the intervention of the conciliator is mandatory only in the case of public utility services. In other cases it is optional depending upon the discretion of the Conciliation Officer to commence the proceedings either in case of an existing or apprehended industrial dispute. The main difference in the Indian and the Pakistani law on the subject of industrial disputes is that in India an industrial dispute can be raised by representatives of workmen or any union which need not even be a registered trade union. In Pakistan an industrial dispute as far as the workmen are concerned can only be raised by a collective bargaining agent. Moreover, the two step formula of bilateral negotiation and conciliation proceedings prescribed in Pakistan before resort to a strike action or lock-out does not find a place under the Indian law.

The other main difference between the Indian and the Pakistani law is that the machinery of adjudication of industrial dispute can be set in motion in India only upon a reference by the appropriate government. It is entirely for the government to decide about the factual existence of a dispute or its apprehension and the expediency of making a reference. The existence of industrial dispute or its apprehension is a subjective opinion though the government must act reasonably and not capriciously or arbitrarily. The government cannot be compelled to make a reference since the questions whether it would be expedient to make a reference or not is a matter in the discretion of the government. The government also need not wait until the procedure or the proceedings in conciliation have been completed. Even where parties to industrial dispute applied in the prescribed manner whether jointly or separately for a reference of the dispute to the Board, Court, Labour Court, Tribunal or National Tribunal, the government is not bound to make the reference unless it is satisfied that the persons applying for reference represent the majority of each party. However, while the right to make a reference to the adjudicatory authority depends upon the discretion of the Competent Authority, the right to declare or commence a strike is not dependent upon a particular union's capacity as a CBA as in Pakistan. Strikes are prohibited in matters covered by a settlement and award or during conciliation and adjudicatory proceedings.

In contrast, the Pakistani law provides that any party raising an industrial dispute may take the matter to a Labour Court for adjudication of the dispute. No reference by a government or the exercise of any discretion or the formation of any opinion about the existence of industrial dispute is required under the Pakistani law. However, only the CBA or the employer can raise an industrial dispute. Moreover, this right becomes non-existent where Wage Commissions are set up under the law for bank, insurance and other financial institutions and their Awards continue to remain in force till a second Wage Commission is set up during which period no industrial dispute can be raised. The same situation prevails in respect of the award of the Wage Boards of newspaper employees.

Through an amendment of section 11-A of the Indian Industrial Disputes Act 1947, the Labour Court, Tribunal or National Tribunal have been empowered to set aside the order of discharge or dismissal and direct reinstatement of a workman on such terms and conditions as it thinks fit on satisfaction that the order of discharge or dismissal was not justified. Previously the law in India and Pakistan limited the jurisdiction of the Labour Courts, etc. only to an examination, as to whether the domestic enquiry was fair or proper, whether there was want of good faith or there was victimization or unfair labour practice on the part of employer. Further, was the management guilty of basic error or violation of principles of natural justice or the findings of enquiry officer were completely baseless or perverse (*Indian Iron and Steel Company Limited vs. their workmen*).

While enlarging the jurisdiction of the Tribunal to determine the justification of discharge or dismissal, the amendment in the Indian law restricts the adjudicatory process to the materials already on record and prohibits taking of any fresh evidence on the matter.

In Pakistan the matter is to be dealt with under section 25-A IRO where the courts have been given the powers to go into all the facts of the case. In the case of Crescent Jute Products (PLD 1978 Supreme Court 207) it was held that the Labour Court has the jurisdiction to go behind a dismissal order to see for itself as to whether on the facts and circumstances of the concerned case were justified or not both on merits as well as law. The Labour Court has full power to enter even into question of fact and to arrive at its own conclusion regardless of there being no illegality of procedure in the domestic proceedings. The only pre-requisite for invoking the jurisdiction of the Labour Court in case of dismissals, retrenchment, termination or in case of any other violation of guaranteed rights is the service of a grievance notice by the workman concerned upon the employer within the period of limitation prescribed under the law.

Under the Indian law even though the definition of industrial dispute has been enlarged to include the dispute of an individual worker and the jurisdiction of the industrial courts have been wildered to look into the justification of the orders of discharge dismissal etc., and to include reinstatement in case of unjustified termination or dismissal etc., the matter still depends upon the reference of the dispute to the adjudicatory authority by the appropriate government, which reference can also be made only after the grievance settlement authority had decided the dispute of an individual workman and its decision is not acceptable to any of the parties to the dispute. Another significant provision added to the Industrial Disputes Act in India was with respect to the liability of the employer to pay to the worker his full wages where he had been reinstated by the orders of a Labour Court or Industrial Tribunal and the matter had been taken to the High Court or the Supreme Court by the concerned employer.

In recent years in Pakistan, the adjudication of individual disputes of workmen in respect of dismissal, discharge or retrenchment have far outnumbered the adjudication of industrial disputes raised by trade union with respect to terms and conditions of employment of workmen. The machinery provided under the IRO for the enforcement of rights guaranteed to workmen under the law, settlement or award is not available to a registered trade union even where it is the collective bargaining agent. This has been confined only to individual workmen, who can however authorize a CBA union to represent their individual grievance under section 25-A of IRO: An anomalous position has been created by the judgement of Supreme Court where even though the collective bargaining agent alone can enter into a settlement but is held to be debarred from moving the Labour Court to enforce it. It is respectfully submitted that the decision of the Supreme Court needs to be reviewed at an appropriate time, particularly keeping in view the fact that a settlement or award does not and cannot confer any right upon the CBA or the trade union as distinct and separately from the workers, since both the award and settlement relates to the determination or adjudication of the terms and conditions of employment of workmen. Since the CBA or the trade union could not have 'its' own terms and conditions of employment, the interpretation given to the word 'it' so as to exclude the CBA from enforcing the rights of the workers and to limit it only to the enforcement of its own rights is too narrow, and self-contradictory.

The narrow grammatical construction put on the provisions of section 34 of IRO by the courts in Pakistan has greatly curtailed the scope for the enforcement of guaranteed rights under a settlement, award or law by the CBA. While on the one hand, the amendment in the definition of the term 'Industrial Dispute' itself excludes matters relating to the enforcement of guaranteed rights, the CBA cannot raise a dispute about the enforcement of rights leaving the matter to individual workers, and curtailing the rights of the CBA and denying a role to it.

In India, exclusion from the law on the formation of trade unions and the settlement of industrial disputes is in-built in the given definition of the term 'workman' and the term 'industry'. The definition of the term workman under the Indian law excludes a person who is subject to the Army Act 1950, Air Force Act 1950 or Naval Disciplines Act 1937 or who is employed in the police service or is an officer or employee of a prison. The definition of the term industry excludes any activity of the government relatable to sovereign functions only; even employees falling within the category of civil servants have not been denied the right to form trade unions or raise industrial disputes. Instances are: 1983 (31) BLJR: where the Irrigation Department of the government of Bihar was declared an industry and temporary tehsildars seasonally employed in the Irrigation Department were held to be workmen by the Patna High Court 1983 (33) PLR 620. The Madras High Court held that Council of Scientific and Industrial Research was not an industry for the purpose of Industrial Disputes Act but was covered by the Trade Unions Act 1926 (1976 FLR 266).

Subsequent to the decision of the Supreme Court of India in the case of Bangalore Water Supply and Sewerage Board in 1978 (36) FLR 266 the Indian Industrial Disputes Act has been amended by the legislature. By virtue of Industrial Disputes (Amendment) Act 1982, the definition of industry has been substituted by a new definition, which specifically includes any activity of dock labour board, and an activity relating to promotion of sales or business and specifically excludes the following activity:

- agricultural operation except activity on plantations;
- hospitals and dispensaries;
- educational, scientific or research institutions;
- institutions owned or managed by organizations wholly or substantially engaged in charitable, social or philanthropic service;
- khadi or village industries;
- government activity relatable to sovereign function including all activities carried on by the departments of Central Government dealing with defence research, atomic energy or space;

- any domestic service;
- any activity being a profession practiced by an individual, if the number of persons employed by the individual or body of individuals in relation to such profession is less than ten;
- any activity carried on by the co-operative society, or a club or any other like body of individuals, if the number of persons employed in relation to such activity is less than ten.

Why should agricultural operations other than plantations be excluded from labour law is not easy to explain except as a measure of political expediency when the reality is that agricultural labour in India is subject to extreme exploitation. Similarly, it is known that large number of hospitals and dispensaries are running on commercial lines; there is no justification either for excluding charitable and philanthropic institutions or those engaged in social service, since charity must always begin at home and the workmen of these institution should not be deprived of fair and reasonable terms and conditions of employment.

The definition also sets at rest many controversies of the past years by enacting that 'industry means any systematic activity carried on by co-operation between an employer and his workmen (whether such workmen are employed by such employer directly or by or through an agency including a contractor) for the production, supply or distribution of goods or services with a view to satisfy human wants or wishes (not being wants or wishes which are merely spiritual or religious in nature), whether or not

— any capital has been invested for the purposes of carrying on such activity; or
— whether or not such activity is carried on with a motive to make profit or not.

The above act also re-defines 'workman' and substitutes a comprehensive definition as under:

Workman means any person (including an apprentice) employed in any industry to do any manual, unskilled, skilled, technical, operational, clerical or supervisory work for hire or reward, whether the terms of employment are express or implied.

Supervisors drawing wages of more than 1600 per mensum and those carrying on functions of or employed in a managerial or administrative capacity are specifically excluded besides persons employed in police service, service in a prison or those subject to Air Force Act, the Army Act or the Navy Act.

Other controversies relating to pre-dominant activities of an establishment, determining its nature as an industry have been taken care of in the new definition of industrial establishment or undertaking which has been defined to mean an establishment or undertaking where an industry is carried on, but the test of severability is laid down. It is thus provided that:

If any unit or establishment or undertaking carrying on any activity, being an industry, is severable from the other unit or units of such establishment or undertaking such unit will be deemed to be a separate industrial establishment or undertaking and where the pre-dominant activity is an industry, and the other unit is not severable, then the entire establishment will be deemed to be an industry.

The 'severability' test laid down by the Supreme Court of India in the Bangalore Water Board case has been thus accepted in India. It may be interesting to note that the definition of the term workman under the Industrial Disputes Ordinance 1968 was in similar terms including within it the category of 'technical workers'.

11 THE LAW OF TERMINATION/ DISMISSAL, RETRENCHMENT, LAY–OFF AND CLOSURE

THE LAW OF TERMINATION/DISMISSAL

The law on termination/dismissal has been the subject matter of unabated controversy between the employers on the one hand and the industrial workers and their unions on the other. The employers and their organizations have been demanding the unrestricted right of 'hire and fire', meaning thereby that the employers should have complete freedom in the matter of employment as well as termination. No reasons should be required to be given for termination of service and they should not be answerable to anybody. The union and the workmen have consistently claimed that termination of service should not be a matter of sweet will of the employer.

In the early years of industrial disputes, legislation and till very late, the right of the employers in this respect was subjected to only some very formal restraints in India. The termination or dismissal of a workman could be taken up or referred as an industrial dispute only if a union or body of workmen sponsored the cause of the individual workman. Standing alone, the aggrieved workman could not get any redress. Secondly, neither the union nor the body of workmen could approach the Industrial/Labour Court directly. It rested with the appropriate government to make the reference of an industrial dispute with respect to termination or dismissal for adjudication to an industrial tribunal. Its discretion in the matter was more or less absolute. In case the dispute was not so referred, the only course open to the unions or body of workers was to go on strike, which was naturally not possible in all cases and recourse to it would be taken only if the matter affected a large number of workers. Thirdly, even where the appropriate government did make a reference of such a dispute for adjudication to a tribunal, its jurisdiction was limited only to the question of law and natural justice.

The industrial courts had very limited jurisdiction to interfere with the 'power of the management to direct its own affairs', internal administration and discipline. When a dispute arose, the industrial tribunal had only the powers to see whether the termination of services of a workman was justified and to give appropriate relief. In case of dismissal for misconduct, the Tribunal however did not act as a Court of Appeal and could not substitute its own judgement for that of the management. It interfered:

— when there was want of good faith;
— when there was victimization or unfair labour practice;
— when the management was guilty of a basic error or violation of the principles of natural justice; and
— when on the materials the finding was completely baseless or perverse (*Indian Iron and Steel Co. vs. their workmen*, AIR1958 SC 150)

The same view of law prevailed in Pakistan till 1972 when section 25-A was added to the IRO and which enabled labour courts to 'go into all the facts of the case' of termination/ dismissal or retrenchment and to pass such orders as it deemed fit in the circumstances of the case.

This development and the said change in the law was noticed by the Supreme Court of Pakistan in the case of *Crescent Jute Products vs. Muhammad Yakub* (PLJ 1978 SC 430) in the following words:

... It is clear that the Labour Court has jurisdiction to go behind a dismissal order and see for itself whether on the facts and circumstances of the concerned case it was justified or not, both on merits as well as law. These words (shall go into all the facts of the case) clearly signify that when a case is brought before a Junior Labour Court, the scope of enquiry is wider than for example the scope of a Tribunal examining only the legality of an order impugned before it. The Labour Court has complete powers to enter even into questions of fact and arrive at its own conclusion regardless of there being no illegality of procedure in the domestic proceedings. The intention of the legislature appears to be to provide a double check in the form of a domestic enquiry to be held by the employer and the other in the form of judicial determination by the Junior Labour Court itself.

By an amendment of Standing Orders Ordinance in S.O.12(3) it was made incumbent upon the employer to pass a written order of termination stating the reasons for the termination of service and the aggrieved workman became entitled as a matter of right to file an application before the Labour Court challenging the said termination whereafter the provisions of section 25-A IRO would become applicable and Labour Court could go into all the facts of the case and pass such orders as it deemed fit and proper in the circumstances of the case. These provisions were applicable both to temporary as well as permanent workmen. This was indeed a major breakthrough in protecting the security of service of an industrial worker.

The right of a dismissed worker to seek relief of reinstatement and get a redressal of his grievance, has recently been jeopardized by a decision of the Supreme Court of Pakistan reported in 1994 SCMR 2213. The Supreme Court, relying on the definition of 'workman' contained in the IRO 1969 and taken over from its definition under the Industrial Disputes Act 1947, held that a dismissed workman could not approach the Labour Court unless an industrial dispute has been raised against his dismissal or his dismissal has led to an industrial dispute. The decision ignores that under the scheme of law in Pakistan and the amended definition of 'industrial dispute,' a matter relating to a right under any law, settlement or award could not be raised as an industrial dispute at all. Whereas an application under section 25-A IRO was necessary for the enforcement of a right guaranteed under the law, settlement or award. The judicial task of reconciling the two apparently contradictory provisions of law could have been undertaken by the courts if the directions of law would have been kept in mind that the application under section 25-A was to be dealt by the Labour Courts as an industrial dispute. The Supreme Court decision in 1998 SCMR 644 now confines the right of redressal in respect of termination/dismissal to workers covered by the Standing Orders Ordinance 1968. Others not thus covered are now denied this right. A decision of the Bombay High Court, reported as AIR 1956 Bombay 30, appears to have taken a more reasonable view on a similar definition of workman under section 2(s) of Indian Industrial Disputes Act 1947, when it held that, 'the definition of workman in section 2(s) does not seem to indicate that the workman must be employed at a particular moment of time. It means any persons who is employed at any time in an industry.' AIR 1957 SC 264 has also held that a person who was once in employment could come within the definition of workman after termination.

By an amendment of Industrial Disputes Ordinance in India in 1956 section 2-A was introduced which enabled even an individual to raise an industrial dispute with respect to his termination and it was no longer necessary for a body of workmen or a union to sponsor his cause. Yet another amendment, section 11-A in the Industrial Disputes Act enabled the Industrial Tribunals and Labour Court to examine the justification of the order of termination/dismissal and set aside the order of dismissal, discharge, order reinstatement or award lesser punishment. The jurisdiction of the Labour Courts/Industrial Courts were thus extended beyond the mere examination of the legality of the order of termination/dismissal. But this examination could not go beyond the records and no new evidence was allowed to be recorded. The Pakistani law on the jurisdiction of the courts/tribunals to examine justification of the orders of dismissal by the employer and grant relief have come closer to the Indian law with the machinery for invoking the jurisdiction more readily available in Pakistan.

In India before an individual could raise the matter of his termination/dismissal as an industrial dispute, resort was necessary to a Grievance Settlement Authority, required to be set up by every employer. Only after the Authority had dealt with the matter, and if any party was aggrieved, the matter could be referred for adjudication. Thus the discretion of the government to refer a dispute for adjudication of an industrial dispute in relation to orders of termination/dismissal of a worker has remained unchanged in India in relation to other matters constituting an industrial dispute.

THE LAW OF RETRENCHMENT, LAY-OFF AND CLOSURE

Retrenchment had not been originally defined in the Industrial Disputes Act 1947 under the Indian law or in the West Pakistan Standing Orders Ordinance 1968. The Supreme Court of India in the case of *Barsi Light Railway vs. Joglekar and others* had held that 'retrenchment means the discharge of surplus labour or staff by the employer for any reason whatsoever, otherwise than as a punishment inflicted by way of disciplinary action'. Similarly, the Bombay High Court, in a case reported as 1962 PLC 1176 held that it will amount to retrenchment if termination of service was found to be due to the reason that the workmen discharged were surplus i.e. in excess of the requirement of business. Similarly, it was held in 1961 PLC 407 that retrenchment could take place only in a continuing business and termination of services of workmen on the closure of the entire business would not fall within the meaning of retrenchment. However, in India by Act 43 of 1953 retrenchment was defined to mean 'the termination of service of a workman by the employer for *any reason* whatsoever, otherwise than as a punishment by way of disciplinary action, but excluding voluntary retirement or termination on ground of continued ill health, or retirement on reaching the age of contractual superannuation.' The pre-condition for retrenchment was laid down as one month's notice or notice pay and payment of compensation at the rate of fifteen days average pay for every completed year of service or part thereof in excess of six months. The notice of such retrenchment had to be given in the prescribed manner. The provision was applicable to workers with at least one-year service in an establishment employing 100 and more workers.

In the case of workmen of Subong Tea Estate, it was held that '...the right of employer to effect retrenchment cannot normally be challenged but when there is a dispute with regard to the validity of the retrenchment, it will be necessary to consider whether retrenchment was justified for proper reasons.' (1964) I LLJ 333(SC).

In Pakistan, it has been held that retrenchment is the discretion of the employer but must be *bona fide* and not to victimize employees or to get rid of particular employees (1981 PLC 24). It has also been held in a case where the employer gave the twisting section on contract and terminated the services of permanent workmen that the order of termination could only be challenged validly if it can be shown to be either *mala fide* or in contravention of any law (1981 PLC 981 SLAT).

It is hard to agree with the above view that validity of retrenchment can only be challenged if it is in violation of some law, since the Supreme Court decision (PLJ 1978 SC 430) emphasizes that the scope of enquiry in a case brought before the Labour Court is not limited to a question of law but the Labour Court can go into all the facts of the case and act as a Court of Appeal both on facts and law. The decision also loses sight of the position that section 25-A (IRO) has been incorporated in Standing Order 12(3) of the Standing Orders Ordinance 1968 (vide PLD 1998 SC 644) which entitles a workman aggrieved by his dismissal or termination to approach the Labour Court whereafter provisions of section 25-A IRO become applicable. The grievance under Standing Orders 12(3) of the Standing Orders Ordinance is not limited to a right guaranteed under any law, settlement or award.

It may be advantageous to bear in mind the observations of Justice Gajendragadkar of the Indian Supreme Court reported in 1961 PLC 95 to the effect that:

> When dealing with the question of retrenchment, the Industrial Tribunal has to consider its two aspects viz. (i) was the employer justified in coming to the conclusion in exercise of its management functions that a certain number of workmen had to be retrenched and (ii) if yes, has the retrenchment been properly carried out.

The trend of judicial decisions in Pakistan appears to be to exclude the first question from consideration altogether on the plea that it was within the management's exclusive functions or discretion. But the scheme of industrial law that has developed in India and Pakistan had tended to restrict the scope of management discretion which is not immune from judicial examination of the justification of decision taken adversely affecting to workers. The Supreme Court of India, in a case reported in 1984 (48) FLR 364 has noted that there have been a change in the very concept of management functions and where it affects large number of workers or society at large, provides for a judicial intervention. The result and consequences of the restricted view taken in Pakistan can be seen in the massive downsizing in the banks and other commercial and industrial establishments in that country in recent times going unchallenged and without any judicial examination of their justification.

The law in India in respect of lay-off and retrenchment is divided into two parts. The first part (under chapter V-A) relates to industrial establishments employing more than fifty workmen and provides for compensation in case of lay-off and retrenchment. Compensation is payable at the rate of one half of the basic wages and dearness allowance in case of lay-off not exceeding 45 days in a period of twelve months. At the end of this period, the lay-off may continue in agreement between the employers and the workmen or the employers may retrench the workers, provided however that the lay-off compensation may be set off against any retrenchment compensation payable to the workers under the law. The entitlement to lay-off compensation is also subject to the laid-off workers accepting alternative employment in the same establishment or in any other establishment belonging to the same employer lying within a radius of five miles from the original establishment.

In case of retrenchment, one month's notice or notice pay *in writing stating the reason for retrenchment* and a retrenchment compensation at the rate of fifteen days average pay for every completed year of continuous service or any part thereof in excess of six months and a notice in writing on the appropriate Government or such Authority as may be specified, is necessary in the Martial Law.

In the case of transfer of an undertaking in respect of ownership or management, the workers are entitled to the same rate of compensation as in the case of retrenchment unless the service of workmen are not interrupted by such a change of ownership or management and the terms and conditions of his service after transfer are not less favourable than those applicable immediately before the transfer and the period of continuity of service of such workmen is not deemed to be interrupted by such transfer.

In case of closure of an undertaking, at least sixty days notice prior to the intended closure is required to be given to the prescribed authority by the employer stating clearly the reasons for the intended closure. The requirement of two months prior notice may be waived by the appropriate authority for reasons like accident in the undertaking, death of the employer and reasons of a like nature.

Compensation is payable to the workers in such an undertaking who are entitled to the same notice pay or pay in lieu thereof in addition to the compensation at the same rate and the same conditions of not less than one year continuous employment as in the case of retrenchment. In case of closure due to unavoidable circumstances, such compensation is not to exceed three months average pay.

Chapter V-B of the Industrial Disputes Act is applicable to establishments employing not less than 300 workmen employed on an average.

In case of lay-off in such an establishment, previous permission of the specified authority is required except in cases of shortage of power or natural calamity. Permission is to be granted or refused by the Appropriate Authority within a period of two months of making the application and shall be deemed to have been granted at the expiry of two months if the Authority does not communicate its decision. In case no application for permission is made, workers shall be entitled to all the benefits as if they had not been laid-off.

In case of retrenchment under the chapter applicable to establishments employing not less than 300 workmen, three months notice in writing or payment in lieu thereof is required to be given to the workmen as well as to the specified authority for permission for retrenchment. Compensation is payable to the workers at the time of retrenchment at the rate of fifteen days average pay for every completed year of continuous service or any part thereof in excess of six months. The appropriate authority is required to give its decision on the application for permission within a period of three months and if no decision is given on the application within this period, it shall be deemed to have been granted. In case no application is made for permission to retrench or permission is refused, workmen shall be entitled to all the benefits under the law as if no notice of retrenchment had been given.

The requirement of ninety days notice or payment of notice pay in lieu thereof to the workers and prior permission of the Appropriate Authority in case of intended closure and other provisions as in the case of intended retrenchment are applicable. Both in case of intended retrenchment and intended closure, the Appropriate Authority is required to make such enquiry as it deems fit on receipt of the notice or application from the employer. The Government or the Appropriate Authority may reject the application for permission to retrench for reasons to be recorded in writing. In case of rejecting the application for closure if the reasons given by the employer are not adequate or prejudicial to public interest.

Retrenchment, under the Indian law has come to mean (by an amendment introduced in 1953, Act 4 of 1953) 'the termination by the employer of the services of a workman for any reason whatsoever, otherwise than as a punishment imposed by way of disciplinary action but does not include (a) voluntary retirement of workmen (b) termination on ground of superannuation provided for in the contract of employment or for continued ill health or expiry of a Contract of Service.'

A consequence of the amendment in the definition of the term retrenchment would mean that all cases of termination of service except in case of dismissal, superannuation, voluntary retirement and continuous ill health would require:

1. Notice or pay in lieu thereof of one month in case of smaller establishment and three months in case of establishments employing 300 or more workmen;
2. Notice in writing of the reasons for such termination;
3. Compensation equal to 15 days wages for every completed year of service;
4. Permission from specified authority for all termination in case of larger establishments.

By virtue of section 11-A of the Industrial Disputes Act 1947 the Industrial Courts have been vested with the jurisdiction to examine the justification and correctness of the management decisions and set aside the orders with consequential benefits. No fresh evidence is however permissible and orders have to be based on the evidence of records.

In Pakistan, by an amendment in the Standing Orders Ordinance by way of insertion of a new section 11-A, it became necessary for an establishment to secure the permission of the Labour Court for closing down the whole establishment or terminating 50 per cent of its workmen. However, no guidelines were laid down for the Labour Court to decide the merits of the application and no machinery was evolved like it was done in

India to examine the contention of the employer that it could not continue to run the establishment or the industry, with the result that no effective protection is afforded against arbitrary or unjustified closure.

12 THE LAW ON UNFAIR LABOUR PRACTICE

While the legislature has accepted the right of association of the workers in the form of trade union rights and their right of collective bargaining with regard to the terms and conditions of employment in the form of their right to raise and pursue industrial disputes, unfair labour practices may be described as those practices which the employers and the workers are prohibited from resorting to in respect of the others' right of association or the right to raise and pursue industrial disputes. These may also be described as practices in restraint of the rights of free association of trade union and the right of raising industrial disputes or collective bargaining and to use unfair and coercive measures to change worker's terms and condition of employment to their advantage or disadvantage on the part of workers or the employers as the case may be.

Under the Indian Law the Industrial Disputes (Amendment) Act 1982 defined unfair labour practice and for the first time provided penalty for resorting to such undesirable practices. The voluntary code of discipline laid down by the Indian Labour Conference suggesting a list of such unfair labour practices was followed in the Indian law which were made punishable with imprisonment for a term which may extend to six months and with fine which may extend to Rs. 1000 or with both. Unfair labour practice on the part of the employer under the Indian law is quite extensive and includes:

— threatening the workmen with discharge or dismissal or with lock-out or closure;

— granting wage increases at crucial periods of trade union organization with a view to undermine the efforts of such organization;
— employer taking active interest in organizing a trade union of his workmen, to establish employer-sponsored trade union of workmen;
— discriminating against any workman;
— discharging or dismissing workmen by way of victimization and in colourable exercise of the employer's rights.

The list also includes some important acts which were earlier claimed to be the management's prerogative. Thus, abolishing a work of regular nature and giving such work to contractors as a measure of breaking a strike and *employing workmen as 'badlies', casuals or temporaries and to continue them as such for years with the objective of depriving them of the status and privileges of permanent workmen are very important elements of unfair labour practice taken note of by the Indian law* on the subject which could be adopted in Pakistan with advantage. Failure to implement an award, settlement or agreement were also included in a comprehensive list of unfair labour practice on the part of the employers. The Indian law declared 'active support or instigation of any strike deemed to be illegal as unfair labour practice on the part of workmen and trade unions of workmen. The list also included picketing as unfair labour practice on the part of the trade unions or its members if it physically debarred the non-striking workmen from entering into the workplace. Indulging in acts of force or violence or holding threats or intimidation in connection with strike against non-striking workmen or against managerial staff, go slow, squatting on the work premises after working hours or '*gherao*' of the members of the managerial staff and to stage demonstration at the residence of the employer or the managerial staff members, wilfully damaging the employer's property connected with the industry, etc. were some of the other unfair labour practices on the fare of workmen or the trade unions.

Under the Pakistani law, unfair labour practice on the part of employer includes:

a. imposition of a condition in the contract of employment restraining a person to join a trade union or to continue his membership of such a trade union;
b. refusal to employ or continue to employ any person or discriminate against any person on the ground that he is or is not a member of a trade union;
c. dismissal, discharge, removal from employment or transfer or injury in respect of employment on the ground that a workman is or proposes to become or persuade others to become members of a trade union;
d. compelling an officer of a collective bargaining agent to enter into a settlement by intimidation, threat, pressure, etc.;
e. recruiting any new workman during the period of notice of strike or during the currency of strike or closing down the whole of establishment without prior permission of the Labour Court;
f. dismissal of the officer of a trade union during the pendency of an application for registration in contravention of section 8-A IRO without the prior permission of the Registrar of Trade Unions, etc.

Acts of unfair labour practice whether on the part of the workmen or employers carry with them stringent punishments of imprisonment up to three years or with fine of two thousand rupees or both. In the case of workers, the officer of a trade union or any other person who contravenes or acts in compelling or attempting to compel an employer to accept any demand by coercion, threat, pressure, assaults, physical injury or confinement (usually described in short as *gherao*) is also liable to be debarred from holding any post in the trade union for one year besides the year in which he is so debarred.

Unfair labour practice on the part of workman in Pakistan include, besides the above mentioned acts of threats, intimidation, coercion, pressure, confinement, ouster, assault and physical injury to the employer for acceptances of their demand, the following:

a. Persuading a workman to join or refrain from joining a trade union during working hours;
b. Commencing or continuing or encouraging an illegal strike or go-slow;
c. Intimidating or inducing any person by conferring of any advantage to become or cease to be member of a trade union.

The word 'pressure' occurring in the definition of unfair labour practice under the Pakistani law was interpreted very widely to cover even moral pressure or any kind of agitation to support the demands of the workers. This was in the spirit of the Martial Law rule in the country. However, the superior courts and even later rulings of the National Industrial Relations Commission did not support this interpretation.

In 1978 PLC 328 it was held that the words intimidation, coercion, pressure, threat or confinement indicated the use of objective forces or pressure to have some physical impact on the employer. Hunger strike being an act of self-infliction and self-immolation could be held to be culpable in the legal sense but not covered by the term 'pressure' which has to be, in order to be culpable, physical by the show of physical restraint or process of a compression or compulsion.

In another case cited as 1978 PLC 326 it was held that the workers did not commit any unfair labour practice in refusing to obey the order to discontinue a strike which was passed without jurisdiction in a case under section 45 IRO in the absence of the pendency of an industrial dispute.

In 1990 PLC 540 the NIRC rejected the contention of the employers that the circulation of the posters showing intention to stage a peaceful march towards the Governor's House and Martial Law Head Quarters with the intention merely to ventilate their grievances and to arouse the demonstration to a sense of realization of such grievance remaining unattended for one and a half year was not an unfair labour practice or a culpable act. It was held that if trade unionism has to stay, they have to be conceded their right to hold peaceful meetings and to ventilate their grievances in all possible peaceful manner. The term 'agitation' also came to be interpreted in the context of unfair labour practice in India.

It was held by the Indian Supreme Court in a case cited as AIR 1975 Supreme Court 228 that: 'It is in our opinion, wrong to treat every agitation as implying violence on a prior consideration.' The High Court of Bombay in a case cited as *Federation of West India Sign Employees vs. Finlay Private Limited* has held as under:

A trade union is entitled to carry out its legitimate trade union activities peacefully and therefore per se shouting or demonstrations could not be termed as unlawful and a blanket injunction cannot be granted. Trade unionism is a universally recognized phenomena. The law has recognized the existence of a trade union as well as the scope and the ambit of the legitimate activities. Needless to say that the expression workman in this context must include ex-workman.

Agitation is defined to mean the persistent and sustained attempt to arouse, to voice or influence public opinion (as by polls, discussion or demonstrations) ... To agitate is to call attention to by speech or writing, discussion, debate to arouse or attempt to arouse public interest as in some political or social questions.

Agitation accordingly means persistent urging of a political or social question before the public.

This is not to say that the trade union is also protected from violent activities. The activities which are normally termed as violent cannot be recognized as legitimate trade union activities of a union.... The union is entitled to carry out its legitimate trade union activities peacefully and therefore per se, slogans or demonstrations cannot be termed as unlawful and hence blanket injunction cannot be granted in that behalf.

It was held in AIR 1962 SC 1166 that 'broadly stated, demonstration is manifestation of the feelings or sentiment of an individual or group. It is thus a communication of ideas to others to whom it is intended to be conveyed. It is in effect therefore a form of speech or expression because speech need not be vocal since signs by a dumb person would also be a form of speech. It would come within the freedom guaranteed by the Constitution. Violent and disorderly demonstration would be obviously not within the freedom under Article 19(1)(a) or (b) but peaceful and orderly demonstration can be within the freedom guaranteed under these clauses.'

In Pakistan, National Industrial Relations Commission (NIRC) has been constituted as a special forum under the law under section 22-A to E of IRO to try offences of unfair labour practice punishable under section 53(1-A). The NIRC has also been empowered to take measures to prevent an employer or workmen from committing unfair labour practice. Rule 32 of the NIRC regulations provide for holding an enquiry where unfair labour practice is likely to occur, to ascertain the factors which are likely to give rise to them, advice, or direct any of the connected persons to act in a manner calculated to avoid occurrence of unfair labour practice, reprimand or warn any of the connected person and initiate security proceedings in order to prevent the occurrence of unfair labour practice.

The NIRC, in apprehended cases of unfair labour practice may pass prohibitory orders and where the prohibitory orders are contravened or violated proceed under section 22-C to punish any person for disobedience of any of its orders or directions. Punishment for such disobedience constituting contempt of court extends to simple imprisonment for six months and fine up to Rs. 2000 or both. The other functions of the NIRC are partly advisory and partly administrative pertaining to the functions of the Registrar of industry-wise trade unions in registering them and holding of ballot. Industry-wise trade unions have been defined as unions the membership of which extend to establishments in more than one province.

The whole concept and constitution of NIRC and powers conferred upon it have come in for serious criticism and objections, on the part of the workers and sometimes even on the part of the employers. The NIRC is constituted mostly of members who do not belong to the judiciary at any level. Even the requirement of the chairman being a retired High Court judge has been diluted so that now the chairman of the NIRC can be a person qualified to be a High Court Judge. It is widely complained that NIRC, constituted of members belonging to the bureaucracy has gone against the promise held out in the 1969 Labour Policy Statement of 'reducing administrative interference in the affairs and function of trade union.' The vast powers of passing ad-interim orders of stay given to the NIRC have been abused in contravention of repeated rulings of the superior courts as in the Karachi and the Lahore High Court. Cases have been known where statutory functionaries like the Conciliator have been prohibited from exercising their mandatory duties under the statute, crippling the bargaining capacity of the unions and prohibiting negotiation or even conciliation proceedings. The definition of industry-wise trade unions and the powers given to the NIRC to determine CBAs at the national level have led to overlapping and fake industry-wise unions replacing powerful local unions enjoying overwhelming massive local support. A body combining judicial, administrative as well as advisory functions like the NIRC has given rise to apprehension of its further misuse and demand of its abolition or replacement by a properly constituted judicial body.

13 THE LAW ON CONTRACT LABOUR

THE LAW ON CONTRACT LABOUR IN INDIA

The employment of contract labour in industry is governed in India by the Contract Labour (Regulation and Abolition) Act 1970, and the central rules under the above law framed in 1971. The main feature of this legislation is the requirement for notified establishments to get themselves registered for the purposes of this Act. Only the principal employer of a registered establishment was entitled to employ contract labour in such establishment. The appropriate government in consultation with the Central Board or a State Board constituted under the Act could prohibit employment of contract labour in any process, operation or other work in any establishment after taking into consideration whether the process, operation or other work was incidental to or necessary for the industry, trade, business, manufacture or occupation carried on in the establishment. The principal nature of the industry and the fact of regular workmen in a establishment or similar establishments carrying on the work, which was given to the contract worker were relevant factors. Thus the power to abolish contract labour was vested in the appropriate government on consideration of the above factors. It was held in the case of *VEGOILS (Pvt) Limited vs. Government* that the decision of the government in this respect was final (1971-II LLJ 567). It was also held in this case that even if the Industrial Tribunal passes an Award abolishing contract labour, it cannot be enforced after the commencement of the Act which had taken away the power of the State Government to refer industrial dispute relating to employment of contract labour to an Industrial Tribunal. The two requirements necessary before ordering abolition of contract labour were held to be:

- The nature of work operated upon by the contract labour must be of a perennial nature that is it must be of sufficiently long duration.
- The operation carried on by contract labour must be incidental to or necessary to the Industry (1974) II LLJ 1970 (AP).

Other provisions of the Act required the licensing of contractors who could undertake or execute any work through contract labour in accordance with the conditions laid down in the license. It was held in the case of *Padam Parshad Jain vs. State of Bihar* reported in 1978 Labour IC 1475 that undertaking or executing any work through contract labour without a license constituted a fresh offense every day on which it continued. The issuance of license was subject to the conditions made under the Contract Labour (Regulation and Abolition) Central Rules 1971 including the stipulation that the rate of wages payable to workmen by the contractor shall not be less than the rates prescribed under the Minimum Wages Act for such employment and where the rates had been fixed by agreement, settlement or award not less than the rates so fixed. The most important condition was that in case where workmen employed by the contractor performed the same or similar kind of work as the workmen directly employed by the principal employer of the establishment, the wage rates, holidays, hours of work and other conditions of service of workmen of the contractor shall be the same as applicable to the workmen directly employed by the principal employer of the establishment on the same or similar kind of work. In other cases the Chief Labour Commissioner had been authorized to specify the wage rates, holidays, hours of work etc., and disagreement about the nature of work was also to be decided by the Chief Labour Commissioner.

The Act appears to invest the Chief Labour Commissioner with wide powers and takes away the power of the unions to raise industrial dispute with respect to abolition of contract labour as per citation above. It is, however, a moot question whether the discretionary exercise of power to prohibit the employment of contract labour was to be exercised judicially and whether the failure to exercise this discretion in judicious manner could be subject to review by the superior courts. The law uses the term 'principal employer' for the owner of the industry. It was held in AIR 1964 Supreme Court page 355 that the persons doing work in an industry, whether the employment was by the management or by the contractor of the management were governed by the term workmen used in the UP Industrial Disputes Act (28 of 1947) and that the owner of the industry was the employer even in respect of workmen employed by a contractor to do the work of the industry. It was held that where the owner of any industry in the course of or for the purposes of conducting the industry contracts with any person for the execution by or under such person of the whole or any part of any work which is ordinarily a part of the industry, the owner of such industry is the employer within the meaning of the Act. It was also held that though the definition of the word workman did not contain any word to show that the contract labour was included that does not affect the position since the definition of workman meant any person including an apprentice employed in any industry to do any skilled or unskilled manual, supervisory, technical or clerical work for hire or reward whether the terms of employment be expressed or implied, were by themselves sufficiently wide to bring in persons doing work in an industry whether the employment was by the management or by the contractor of the management.

It was held in a similar case cited as AIR 1955 Supreme Court 404:

> If a master employed a servant and authorized him to employ a number of persons to do a particular job and to guarantee fidelity and efficiency for a cash consideration, the employees thus appointed by the servant would be equally with the employer, servants of the master.

It was further held that it is not always correct to say that persons appointed and liable to be dismissed by an independent contractor can in no circumstances be the employee of a third party.

The Beedi and Cigar Workers (Conditions of Employment) Act 1966 was challenged before the Supreme Court of India in a case cited as *Manglore Beedi Works vs. Union of India and others*. A full bench of five judges of Supreme Court of India considered whether the Act and the restriction imposed on it violated freedom of trade and business guaranteed under Article 19(1)(g) of the Indian Constitution and whether the Act imposed the conditions which were arbitrarily excessive and extraneous imposing unreasonable restriction on freedom of trade and business. The Supreme Court of India held that the true nature and character of the legislation shows that it was for enforcing better conditions of labour amongst those engaged in manufacture of Beedi and Cigar and were within the legislative constitutional competence. It was held that the liability fastened by the Act was on a person who himself engaged labour or the person for whom and on whose behalf labour is engaged where a person had ultimate control over the affairs of the establishment by reason of advancement of the money. The manufacturer or trade mark holder of master becomes the principal employer and is a real master of the business. He cannot escape liability imposed on him by the Statute by stating that he has engaged labour through contractor to do the work. The contractor in such case employed labour only for and on behalf of the principal employer. It will always be a question of fact in each case as to who is the person for whom or on whose behalf contract labour is engaged.

In the case of *Hussain Bai vs. Altath Factory Cali Cot and others* (1978 II LLJ) 397, the Supreme Court of India held that 'mere contracts are not decisive and the complex of considerations relating to the relationship is different... where a worker or group of workers labour to produce goods and services and these goods or services are for the business of another, that other is in fact the employer. He has economic control over the worker's subsistence, skill and continued employment. If he for any reason chokes off, the worker is virtually laid off.'

It was further held in the same case as:

It is not in dispute that 29 workmen were denied employment which led to the reference. It is not in dispute that the work done by those workmen was an integral part of the industry concerned; that the raw material was supplied by the management; that the factory premises belonged to the management; that the equipment used also belonged to the management; and that the finished product was taken by the management for its own trade. The workmen were broadly under the control of the management where defective article were directed to be rectified by the management. This concatenation of circumstances is conclusive of the question.

The presence of intermediate contractors with whom alone the workers have an immediate contractual relationship is of no consequence, when on lifting the veil, the naked truth is discovered though draped in different paper arrangement; that the real employer is the management and not the intermediate contractor ... Courts should be astute to avoid the mischief and achieve the purpose of law and not be misled by the legal appearances.

The Contract Labour (Abolition and Regulation) Act 1970 came for consideration in two land mark decisions of the Supreme Court of India in the case of *Gujrat Electricity Board vs. Hind Mazdoor Sabha and others* (decided on 9 May 1995) and in the case of *Air India Statutory Corporation vs. United Labour Union and others* (decided on 6 December 1996). In the first case it was held that after the coming into operation of the Act of 1970 the authority to abolish the contract labour vested exclusively in the appropriate government but where there was no genuine contract and the so-called contract was sham or camouflage, the concerned workmen had to raise an industrial dispute for the relief that they should be deemed to be employees of the principal employer.

The Supreme Court of India in the case of Air India Statutory Corporation went further than the above decision and held that,

on abolition of contract labour system under section 10 of the Act, by the appropriate government, the logical and legitimate consequence thereof will be that the erstwhile regulated contract labour covered by the sweep of such abolition for the concerned activities would be entitled to be treated as direct employees on whose establishment they were earlier working ... at least from the day on which the contract labour system gets abolished.

It also held that it is the obligation of the appropriate government to abolish the contract system prevailing in a given process or operation in the establishment once the given conditions are fulfilled namely that the work was of a perennial nature, incidental or necessary to the industry, trade or business etc., done ordinarily through regular workmen sufficient to employ sufficient number of whole time workmen.

Law on Contract Labour in Pakistan

There is no law in Pakistan corresponding to the Indian law on the subject, i.e., the Contract Labour (Abolition and Regulation) Act 1970. The courts in Pakistan have been following the earlier principle laid down in AIR 1968 SC 503 that 'a person must be considered free to so arrange his business so that he avoids a regulatory law and its financial consequences, which without such arrangement, he has no proper means of obeying so long as he does not break that or another law.' Faced with the provisions of Section 20 of West Pakistan Industrial and Commercial Employment Standing Orders where the employer is made liable whether or not the workmen of such establishment are employed through contractor, the Superior Courts in Pakistan made a distinction in a case where the worker was employed though the contractor and where the contractor himself employed workers for carrying out the contract which he has undertaken. A contractor who had contracted to run a petrol pump of a company and not merely to supply labour to be engaged by the company, having powers of hire and fire and assigning work and the manner of serving the customers was held to be the employer and not the company or the factory. So that the Pakistani courts in rare cases have given thought to the 'conceptual confusion between doctrine of law of contract and special branch of law like the labour laws sensitive to exploitative situation.' However, it is yet to be accepted in Pakistani judicial decisions that mere contracts are not decisive and that a complex of considerations relevant to the relationship are relevant.

The Provincial Employees Social Security Ordinance 1965, has tried to go beyond the old concepts by introducing a wide definition for the term 'employer', 'employee' and 'establishment'. The later being defined as 'an organization, industrial, commercial, agricultural or otherwise, the employer or the owner of the industry, business undertaking or establishment in which an employee works', and the 'employee' as a person 'working for wages in or in connection with the work of any industry, business, undertaking or establishment.' This has squarely brought the contractor workers within the network of Social Security Scheme with responsibility for contribution on the owner of the industry.

However, the process of casualization which has set in with massive induction of contract labour in Pakistan requires changes in the labour laws, particularly the Industrial Relations Ordinance and the Standing Orders Ordinance 1968. Section 20 of the later enactment would only need a minor but significant amendment adding the word 'by' or 'through' a contractor, to extend protective and beneficial clauses of the Ordinance to contract workers.

It can be concluded that the purpose behind 'casualization of labour' by way of introduction of contract labour or other means is to reduce or avoid the burdens of social legislation upon the industry in particular of the legal provisions with respect to security of employment, bonus, insurance, and other minimum terms and conditions of employment available to direct workers. The Draft Labour Policy of the present government in Pakistan however, seeks to confer protection upon the system of contract labour on the plea that it has become too widespread for abolition and interference. That would, in fact be tantamount to perpetuating a fraud on the statute, and turning the wheels back on social welfare legislation, whereas in most cases the 'contract' accorded such sanctity, are mere paper arrangements.

Even in the case of Indian legislation on the subject, the discretion conferred upon the appropriate government to abolish the contract system needs to be taken away and substituted by the rule of law as per the Air India case that the 'organization' owning the industry is the employer and any person working for wages in or in connection with the work of an industry, business or establishment is an employee and that such an employer is liable and an employee entitled to the legal benefits under the various regulation and enactments.'

14 THE MINIMUM WAGES LEGISLATION

The concept of a 'living wage' was first put forth in 1907 by Justice Higgins, President of the Commonwealth Court of Conciliation and Arbitration in Australia. It was said that basic wage is the lowest wage which can be paid to unskilled labour on the basis of the normal needs of an employee, regarded as a human being living in a civilized community. A living wage is wage sufficient to ensure to the workman food, shelter, clothing, frugal comfort, and provision for evil days. In another case, Justice Higgins observed that a wage which does not allow of a matrimonial condition and maintenance of about five persons would not be treated as a living wage. According to the South Australian Act of 1912, a living wage means 'a sum sufficient for the normal and reasonable needs of the average employee living in a locality where work under consideration is done.' The Commissioner of the Bureau of Labour Statistics in the United States of America, in 1919 analysed a wage budget with reference to three concepts namely the pauper and poverty level, the minimum subsistence level and the minimum health and comfort level. The Royal Commission on the Basic Wage for the Commonwealth of Australia accepted the description of the minimum health and comfort level which represented a slightly higher level than that of subsistence.

In India, the United Provinces Labour Enquiry Commission classified levels of living standards in four categories, poverty level, minimum subsistence level, subsistence plus comfort level and comfort level and chose the subsistence plus comfort level as the basis of what it called the 'minimum living wage.'

The International Labour Organization has summarized the estimates made in different countries about the amount of a 'living wage'. These estimates can be classified into at least three groups:

- The amount necessary for mere subsistence.
- The amount necessary for health and decency.
- The amount necessary to provide a standard of comfort.

Confronted with the reality, both in India and Pakistan, that prevailing wages even in the organized industry were far lower than a minimum living wage for a family of five calculated on a reasonable basis, the industrial tribunals have taken resort to the concept of fair wages which lay emphasis on the industry-cum-region formulae and wage levels in comparable concerns. When it is said that regard should primarily be had to the rate of wages being paid for similar work, it is presumed that fair wages already exist in some industries in some localities and that the process will suffice to ensure fair wages for labour either in a sweat industry or in an industry where the bargaining power of labour is weak. But application of this formula may very well mean, as far as organized industries are concerned, to maintain either a *status quo* or leave the matter to the strength of collective bargaining.

The establishment of a 'national minimum wage' namely a wage below which no wage earner in the country should be paid was considered by the Central Advisory Board in India in April 1954. The Board decided that in view of difference in economic conditions and the wage levels in various States and regions, provision should be made for fixation of different wage levels on the basis of appropriate area-wise and employment-wise classification.

V.V. Giri in his work 'Indian Industry' writes 'nothing short of a living wage can be a fair wage, if under competitive conditions, an industry can be shown to be capable of paying a full living wage. The minimum wage standards set the irreducible level, the lowest limit or the floor, below which no worker shall be paid.'

The question of fixing a minimum wage came under consideration of the Royal Commission on Labour in India which recommended that the small industries, for example bidi-making, wool-cleaning, mica factories, shellac manufacturing and tanning, should be examined with a view to determining the need and possibility of instituting minimum-wage-fixing machinery. Considerable interest in the subject was also created by the Minimum Wage-Fixing Machinery Convention (No. 25) adopted by the International Labour Conference in 1928. The Minimum Wages Act in India was ultimately passed in 1948 enabling the Central and the State governments to fix minimum wages in what can be termed as the 'sweated' industries. The Minimum Wages Act 1961 was applicable only to scheduled industries enabling the appropriate government to fix or revise the minimum rates of wages consisting of a basic rate of wages plus an allowance according as nearly as practicable with the variation in the cost of living. The procedure in fixing the minimum rates of wages or revising such rates, required the government to appoint enquiry and advisory committees in respect of such fixation or revision and publish its proposals for the information of persons likely to be affected by these proposals and taking into consideration any representations made in this behalf.

The government was also authorized under the Act to fix the number of hours of work which shall constitute a normal working day inclusive of one or more specified intervals, provide for a day of rest in every period of seven days and for payment of remuneration on the rest days and for work on the day of rest at a rate not less than the overtime rate. The government was empowered to fix overtime rates for work beyond the daily or weekly hours of work fixed under this law. Full wages for the day were also ensured when the employer omitted to provide them with work for the whole day. The schedule of employment to which the Act applied were woolen, including carpet-making and shawl-weaving, rice, flour or dal mills, plantations, oil mills, construction, or maintenance of roads, stone-breaking and stone-crushing, lac-manufacture, mica works, tanneries and leather-manufacturing, gypsum, bauxite, kynite, copper and other specified mines except coal and iron ore. The Government of India could add to the list of scheduled industries for the application of this Act. List II of the schedule included agriculture, horticulture, dairy farming etc. where also minimum wages could be fixed by the appropriate government.

In case of fixation of minimum wages, the plea of the employer that he had not got the capacity to pay even minimum wages and is therefore an unreasonable restriction in his fundamental right to carry on business has been repeatedly rejected by the Indian courts including the Supreme Court of India.

EMPLOYEES COST OF LIVING (RELIEF) ACT IN PAKISTAN

In Pakistan the Minimum Wages Legislation has gone beyond the limits of legislation in this field in India. It has not remained confined to sweated or selected industries. The Coal Mines Fixation of Rates of Wages Ordinance was enacted in 1960 which enabled the Provincial Government to fix the minimum rates of wages payable to persons employed in coal mines by notification in the official gazette from time to time and in consultation with an advisory committee constituted under the Coal Mines Labour Welfare Fund Act 1947. The provisions of the Ordinance were in addition to the Industrial Disputes Ordinance 1959 and the Standing Orders Ordinance 1960 and not in derogation thereof and were to have effect notwithstanding anything inconsistent therewith in any award, agreement or contract of service whether made before or after the commencement of this Ordinance.

The Minimum Wages Ordinance 1961 was enacted on 29 September 1961, authorizing the constitution of a Board which could recommend to the government upon a reference made to it, after necessary enquiries, to fix minimum rates of wages for adult unskilled and juvenile workers employed in industrial undertakings in the province where no effective machinery existed for regulating wages. The Board could recommend minimum rates of wages for all classes of workers in any grade and could specify the minimum rates of wages for time work, piece work, overtime work and work on the weekly days of rest and for paid holidays etc. Minimum rates of wages were recommended by the Board for different categories of workers in steel re-rolling industries in West Pakistan, under this enactment ranging from Rs. 350 per month for the managerial and superior supervisory post; Rs. 150 per month for foreman, chargemen, head clerks and steno-typist, for the skilled workers, hammer man, billet feeder it was Rs. 104 whereas for unskilled workers it was Rs. 78 only. Similar recommendations were made for workers employed in sugar industry, leather industry, silk and rayon, plastic products, cotton-ginning industries, woolen textile industries, ice manufacturing, motor, road transport industry, match industry etc by the Wage Board set up in 1964 and 1965.

The Minimum Wages for Unskilled Workmen Ordinance was enacted on 28 August 1969 fixing Rs. 140 per month as minimum wages for unskilled workmen for Karachi and Rs. 110 for other industrial areas. Deduction of Rs. 5 each were allowed if the employer provided housing accommodation or transport. The law saved such award, agreement or contract of service which entitled the workers to higher wages than those under this law with the provision that agreement between workers and employers arrived at under duress between the 1 to 25 March 1969 shall be void and ineffective. This law has been followed by amendments in the federal law raising the minimum wages by statute as well as by provincial government accepting the recommendations of the Minimum Wages Board under the Minimum Wages Act 1961.

The amounts of wages increased by the Employees Cost of Living (Relief) Act were adjustable against increases secured through collectively bargained settlements where it was intended that such increases were given to off-set the increase in the cost of living.

On 1 July 1997, the Sindh Minimum Wage Board recommended to the government, which was accepted and duly notified by it, that the minimum rate of wages for adult unskilled workers would be Rs. 2050 per month of twenty-six days or

Rs. 80 per day of eight hours. This was payable in all industrial undertakings without any reference on the number of workmen employed and was declared to be inclusive of the various increases in minimum wages allowed under the West Pakistan Minimum Wages for Unskilled Workmen Ordinance, the Employees Cost of Living (Relief) Act, and Sindh Employees Special Allowance Act.

15 SOCIAL SECURITY LEGISLATION

Till 1948 the only central legislation in India existing on the issue of social security could be said to be the Workmen's Compensation Act 1923 and Maternity Benefit Act in certain cases. The claim for social security was pressed by the trade union movement in India on the ground that it was fundamental to wage-fixation as an essential element of a worker's living standard and his/her capacity to continue in employment. Since the continuation of the industrial system pre-supposes the re-production of labour power, therefore the necessity of maintaining the worker and his family at a certain level of health and wellbeing through the inevitable incident of sickness, maternity, invalidity, employment injuries, sudden loss of job, old age and death called for a complex of social insurance, besides the recognition of the concept of social justice.

The Employees State Insurance Act was put on the statute book in India in 1948 but was in cold storage till 1952 whereafter it started being implemented in stages. In 1952, the Provident Fund Act was enacted, which was to be applied initially only to six industries viz. textiles, cement, engineering, cigarette, iron and steel and paper industries. In these industries also, the law applied only to larger establishment employing fifty or more workers.

SOCIAL SECURITY LEGISLATION IN PAKISTAN

In Pakistan, Provincial Employees Social Security Ordinance 1965 repealed and replaced the Workmen's Compensation Act 1923, the Employers Liability Act 1938, Mines Benefit Act 1941 and West Pakistan Maternity Benefit Ordinance 1958 in respect of the establishments where the Social Security

Ordinance 1965 was made applicable. The applicability of the Ordinance to specific establishments was subject to the notification of the provincial government. The Ordinance introduced the following benefits:

- Sickness benefit.
- Maternity benefit.
- Death grant.
- Medical care during sickness and maternity.
- Medical care of dependents.
- Injury benefit.
- Disablement pension.
- Disablement gratuity.
- Survivors pension.

Originally the amount of contribution according to the social security contribution rules was 4 per cent of the wages payable by the employers and 2 per cent per day of wages up to and including Rs. 20 per day payable by the workers. For workers drawing wages of less than Rs. 2 per day, the entire contribution of 6 per cent of wages was payable by the employers. By an amendment of 1973, the contribution was raised to 7 per cent of the wages of the workers and the entire contribution became payable by the employers alone. The limit of wages at which contribution was payable was raised to Rs. 40 per day in 1976. Subsequently, the law was amended to bring under the scheme all employees irrespective of the wages with the proviso that contribution of the employer was limited only to that part of the wages which were Rs. 40 per day or less. By the Ordinance called the Labour Laws Amendment Ordinance 1993 employees drawing wages upto Rs. 3000 per month were covered by the scheme and it was provided that an employee would not cease to be an employee for the reason that his monthly wages exceed Rs. 3000. No contribution was payable on so much of employees wages as was in excess of Rs. 120 per day or Rs. 3000 per month.

Wages have the same meaning as under the Payment of Wages Act, that is it includes basic wages and all allowances excepting traveling allowances and allowances paid to defray special expenses and bonus.

Other enactments in the nature of social security in other spheres were as under:

WORKER'S CHILDREN (EDUCATION) ORDINANCE 1972

Ordinance No. XI of 1972 was enacted on 13 April 1972 to provide for the education of workers, children and matters anciliary thereto. Under this Ordinance, every employer of an establishment in which the number of workers employed at any time during a year was ten or more was liable to pay to the provincial government education cess at the rate of Rs. 100 per worker per annum. A establishment included any office, firm, industrial unit, undertaking, shop or premises employing workers for the purpose of carrying on any business, trade or manufacture, calling-service, employment or occupation. A worker was defined to mean any employed person hired to do any skilled or unskilled, manual or clerical work whose monthly wages did not exceed Rs. 1000. Persons in the service of the State including members of the armed forces, police force, railway or any undertaking under the control of any defence organization or railway administration or local council, municipal committee, a cantonment board or any other local authority were exempted. The benefits available to the workers under this Ordinance were the provision of education free of cost up to any level to two children of every worker employed in the establishment. Initially, free education was to be provided by the provincial government to any one child of a worker up to matriculation. This has now been amended so that the Provincial Government is required to provide free education to two children of every worker up to any level. However there does not seem to be any effective machinery for the implementation or carrying out of the requirement under this Act by the Provincial Government.

EMPLOYEES OLD AGE BENEFIT ACT 1976

Under this law, contribution is payable every month by the employer to the EOB Institution in respect of every person in his insurable employment at the rate of 5 per cent of his wages in the prescribed period. The Federal government is also liable to make contribution in respect of every insurable person at the rate of 5 per cent of his wages. No contribution is payable on so much of the wages of an insured person as is in excess of Rs. 3000. No contribution is also payable in respect of an insured person who is in receipt of pension or has attained the age of 60 years and 55 in the case of a woman.

The noticeable feature of this Act is that even clubs, hotels, organizations and messes not maintained for profit or gain and establishments including hospitals for the treatment of the sick, infirm, destitute or mentally unfit persons, a construction industry, a factory as defined in the Factories Act and a mine as defined in the Mines Act and a road transport service are covered. The provisions of the Act are applicable to every industry or establishment employing ten or more persons on any day during the preceding twelve months. Even if the number of employees is reduced to less than ten at any time after the Act became applicable, the industry or establishment would still be liable under the Act. An employee was widely defined as any person employed directly or through any other person for wages or otherwise to do any skilled or unskilled supervisory, clerical, manual or other work in connection with the affairs of the industry or establishment. Employer was also defined widely to include a person who has ultimate control over the affairs of industry or establishment and where these affairs are vested in any other person such as managing agent, managing director, manager, superintendent, secretary or such other persons. Establishment was defined to mean an establishment under the West Pakistan Shops and Establishment Ordinance 1969. Construction industry was defined as in West Pakistan Industrial and Commercial Employment Standing Orders Ordinance 1968. A factory is defined as in the Factories Act, mines are defined as in the Mines Act, a road transport service is as defined in the Road Transport Worker's Ordinance. The qualifying period for entitlement to the various benefits under the Act was dependent upon the age of an insurable person and the number of years for which the contributions were payable. Old Age Pension was payable to a person over the age of sixty years or fifty-five years in the case of a woman and where contributions in respect of him were payable for not less than fifteen years. Where a person in insurable employment was already forty years of age (thirty-five years in case of a woman), the requirement of number of years for which contributions were payable were reduced to seven years and five years. Where the person in insurable employment was forty-five years of age when the Act became applicable, the old age grant became payable on the insured person being in employment for not less than two years for which contributions were payable. The survivor's pension was payable to the surviving spouse of the insured person while in insurable employment had completed at least thirty-six months in insurable employment. The minimum pension in such case was payable for life. An invalidity pension in case of injury was payable to an insured person where contributions in respect of him were payable for not less than fifteen years or since his entry into insurable employment were payable for not less than five years and who was under sixty years of age or under fifty-five years in case of a woman.

Under the schedule, the quantum of old age pension has been revised from time to time.

SOCIAL SECURITY LEGISLATION IN INDIA

The legislation in India relating to Social Security of workmen employed in industries can be classified as under:

1. Employees State Insurance Act 1948 and the Rules 1950.
2. Employees Provident Funds and Miscellaneous Provident Fund Act 1952 and the Employees Provident Scheme 1952.

3. Employees Family Pension Scheme 1971.
4. Employees Deposit-Linked Insurance Scheme 1976.
5. Maternity Benefit Act 1961.
6. Maternity Benefits Miners Rules 1963.
7. Worker's Compensation Act 1923 and Rules 1924.
8. Beedi Workers Welfare Cess Act and Beedi Workers Welfare Fund Act 1976.
9. Coal Mines Provident Fund and Miscellaneous Provident Fund Act and Coal Mines Labour Welfare Fund Act.
10. Employees State Insurance Act 1948 (applies in the first instance to all factories other than seasonal factories and may be extended to any other establishment or class of establishments, industrial or commercial or otherwise; extension of the provisions of this Act to any other establishment or class of establishments etc., can be done by the appropriate government in consultation with the corporation).

The Employees State Insurance Act sets up Employees State Insurance Fund wherein all contribution paid under the Act and all other moneys received on behalf of the corporation are to be paid. All the employees in factories or establishments to which this Act applies are required to be insured under the Act. The principal employer is required to pay in respect of every employee whether directly employed by him or by or through an immediate employer both the employer and the employees' contribution. No employees' contribution was to be payable on behalf of the employee whose average daily wages was Rs. 1.50 (in the year 1966). The employees' contribution can be recovered by the employer by deduction from his wages.

The insurance fund is to be spent only for the purposes specified including the payment benefits, establishment and maintenance of hospitals, dispensaries and other institutions and the provisions of medical treatment and attention to insured person and their families where such a provision is made in respect of their families. The rates of contribution are specified in the schedule to the Act and the employer is required to pay double the contribution payable by the employee. The benefits available under the Act include the following:

1. Sickness Benefits equal to standard benefit rate.
2. Maternity Benefits equal to twice the standard rates.
3. Disablement and Dependents Benefits at Rs. 25 more than the standard rates.
4. Dependents Benefit as in case of the death of the insured person at Rs. 25 more than the standard rates.

On the whole the Social Security benefits are wider in the field of coverage in Pakistan than in India, despite the existence of a stronger trade union movement in the latter country.

PAYMENT OF GRATUITY ACT 1972 (INDIA) AND THE CORRESPONDING PROVISION IN PAKISTAN

This Act, was applicable to an establishment, factory, mine, oil field, plantation, port, railway and every shop and establishment in India employing ten or more employees but covered employees drawing wages of not more than one thousand rupees per month employed to do any skilled, semi-skilled, or unskilled manual, supervisory or technical work but excluding managerial and administrative cadre as also those persons covered under the Army, Air Force and Navy Act. It was, however, applicable to other government employees employed in the commercial establishment or local authorities. An employee completing five years of service or more became entitled under the Indian law to a gratuity of fifteen days for every completed year of service which was not to exceed twenty months wages in any case.

The provision for forfeiture of the claim to gratuity arose only in case of dismissal for riotous or disorderly behavior or any other act of violence or for an offence of moral turpitude committed in course of employment. Where an employee was dismissed for any act of wilful negligence causing damage or loss to the property of the employer, gratuity would be forfeited only to the extent of such damage or loss. Retirement or voluntary resignation after the qualifying period of five years continuous service also entitled an employee to claim gratuity. In Pakistan, provision for gratuity is made for all skilled, unskilled and manual or clerical workers employed in industrial or commercial establishments employing twenty or more workmen. But because the Standing Orders Ordinance is not applicable to establishments carried on by or under the authority of the Federal or Provincial Government having its own statutory rules of service, conduct or discipline, the benefits of gratuity are also not available to them. The rate of gratuity has now been increased to 30 days wages for every year of completed service in excess of 6 months but is to be forfeited in its entirety and not payable in case of worker being dismissed for any misconduct. It is also not available where there is a provision for provident fund.

In fixing the rates of payment both under the Payment of Gratuity Act 1972 and compensation u/s 25-F of the Industrial Dispute Act 1947, the Indian legislature has taken care to define the term wages under both enactment to mean all remuneration including Basic wages, Dearness Allowance, but excluding Bonus, House rent, etc.

BONUS AND PROFIT SHARING SCHEMES IN INDIA AND PAKISTAN

Companies Profits (Workers Participation) Act 1968 receiving the assent of the President of Pakistan on 4 July 1968 was originally intended as a substitute for bonus to provide for 'participation' of workers in the profits of the companies under a schedule which applied the scheme to all companies primarily engaged in industrial undertaking where the number of workers employed in any shift at any time during the year was 100 or more or the paid up capital of the company was two million or more or the value of the fixed assets of the company at cost was four million or more. The benefit of the scheme was limited to persons drawing wages of not more than Rs. 300 per month at the time of its first enactment, which has now been raised to Rs. 3000 per month. Every company was required to set up a fund and pay to the fund annually at the close of its accounting year a sum equal to 2½ per cent of its profits during such year. The scheme as originally framed provided that if a worker voluntarily left the employment of the company before the expiry of three years from the date of his entitlement to the benefits of the scheme, his share in the fund stood forfeited in favour of the fund. The workman voluntarily leaving the employment of the company after completing three years of service was entitled to receive 50 per cent of the net asset value of the units in his name, if he left employment before completing four years; 75 per cent if he left thereafter before completing five year; and 100 per cent of the net asset value of the units standing in his name if he left the employment after five years or more. A worker who was dismissed from service forfeited his share in the fund and a workman in the event of his retirement or his nominated beneficiary in the event of his death while in the employment of the company was entitled to receive 100 per cent of the net asset value of the units. The number of units to the credit of a worker was arrived at by dividing the emolument drawn during the year of account by twelve. But no worker was to receive more than Rs. 1000 (now raised to Rs. 3000) out of annual allocation. The amount left out of the allocation was to be transferred to the Workers Welfare Fund constituted under Ordinance 36 of 1971.

Originally the employees entitled to the benefits of the Scheme were divided into three categories, namely those drawing monthly wages of Rs. 300 those drawing up to Rs. 600 and those drawing up to Rs. 1000. The three categories now are those drawing up to Rs. 1800, 2200, and 3000 respectively.

But the major modification enacted in 1972 is that an employee becomes entitled to 100 per cent of his allocated share every year. The condition of the length of service and its continuity has been done away with; worker's share being available to the company before its distribution and the workers entitlement to convert their assets into shares at the time of new issue of shares has become more or less redundant.

In Pakistan, the provision for minimum bonus is made under the Standing Order 10-C of the West Pakistan Industrial and Commercial Employment Standing Orders Ordinance 1968. In case the amount of profit is not less than the aggregate of one months' wages of workmen employed, profit bonus shall be not less than the amount of such aggregate, subject to a maximum of 30 per cent of such profits. Where profit is less than the aggregate of one month wages, bonus shall not be less than 15 per cent of such profit. It has been held by the Supreme Court of Pakistan that statutory bonus cannot be given in addition to the agreed bonus but to the extent agreed bonus falls short of statutory bonus, employers will have to make good the difference between the two. This provision does not debar the unions from raising an industrial dispute for the payment of bonus over and above the minimum guaranteed under the law.

The Standing Labour Committee of India in March 1960 recommended the appointment of the Bonus Commission with a view to evolving certain norms for the payment of bonus in cash or in deferred payments, which would be helpful in the settlement of bonus disputes. The government appointed a Tripartite Bonus Commission in December 1961, and ultimately the Payment of Bonus Act 1965 was passed which provides for the payment of bonus to persons employed in certain establishments. The Act is applicable to every factory and every other establishment in which twenty or more persons are employed on any day during the accounting year. Where the government intends to apply the Act to a factory or an establishment employing more than ten but less than twenty persons, two months' notice was required to be given of its intention to do so. Every employer was bound to pay every employee in respect of the accounting year commencing 1979 and subsequent accounting years, a minimum bonus equal to 8.33 per cent of salary or wages earned by the employee during the accounting year irrespective of whether the employer had any 'allocable surplus'. Where the allocable surplus exists the employer is bound to pay every employee as bonus an amount in proportion to the salary or wages earned by him during the accounting year subject to a maximum of 20 per cent of such salary or wages. Detailed provisions were made with respect to the calculation of available surplus, allocable surplus and set off against previous losses. Bonus was payable within a period of eight months from the close of the accounting year or within a month from the date of an award or settlement in case of a pending dispute. Dispute between an employer and an employee with respect to the bonus payable or with respect to the application of this Act to an establishment in the public sector was to be deemed to be an industrial dispute under the industrial dispute Act 1947 and has to be adjudicated like any other industrial dispute.

16 Laws of Industrial Employment and Other Specific Industries

The Industrial Employment Standing Order Act in India provided for the framing of Standing Orders in all industrial establishments (including factories, mines, railways, docks and plantations) employing 100 or more workers. It prescribed that, within six months of the application of the Act, the employer shall submit to the Certifying Officer draft standing orders covering matters specified in the schedule to the Act. The Certifying Officer was empowered to modify the draft standing orders so as to render them certifiable under the Act. In the original Act, he had no right to adjudicate upon their fairness, but by an amendment, he has been empowered to enquire into and decide the fairness of the Draft Standing Orders and alter them accordingly. No oral evidence, having the effect of varying or contradicting a Certified Standing Order, shall be admitted in any court. If any question arises to the application or interpretation of a standing order, the same may be referred to the specified Labour Court. Government is also empowered to make model standing orders. The Act provides for consultation of the workers concerned before certification of the Standing Orders framed for any industrial establishment. The government is empowered to exempt, either conditionally or unconditionally, any industrial establishment from all or any of the provisions of the Act.

The West Pakistan Industrial and Commercial Standing Orders Ordinance 1960 was made applicable to industrial as well as commercial establishments employing fifty or more workmen and instead of leaving every establishment to have its own Standing Orders certified by the Certifying Officer in consultation with the workers concerned, provided for statutorily determined Standing Orders concerning recruitment, discharge, disciplinary action, holidays etc. which could be modified by collective agreement only but not to the detriment of any rights given under the Act. The schedule classified the workers as permanent, probationers, *badlies*, casual and apprentices. West Pakistan Industrial and Commercial Standing Orders Ordinance 1968, repealed the 1960 Ordinance and re-enacted the same with some far-reaching amendments. It was also made applicable to commercial establishments employing forty-nine or more workmen.

Significant and wide ranging modifications were made in the Ordinance in 1972 and 1973. A significant change brought about in 1973 made the termination of service of a workman conditional on the employer giving the order in writing and specifying the reasons for such termination. An independent enquiry by an independent Enquiry Officer become mandatory in all cases of dismissal. A worker was required to be informed of the charges against him within one month of the alleged misconduct or the same coming to the knowledge of the employer. The worker proceeded against could get the assistance of a co-worker. Any workman aggrieved by termination of his service for removal, retrenchment, discharge or dismissal could take action in accordance with section 25-A of the IRO for redress.

The amendments of 1972, 1973 also introduced the following benefits namely:

- Gratuity at the rate of fifteen days wages for every completed year of service (further increased to twenty and then thirty days by subsequent amendments) in all cases of termination other than dismissal for misconduct.
- Profit bonus as per details in the chapter on bonus.
- Compulsory group insurance in cases of death and injury arising out of contingencies not covered by Workmen's Compensation Act but on the same scale.

- Prior permission of the Labour Court made compulsory in case of the total closure of the establishment or the termination of more than 50 per cent of workmen employed. Retrenchment was permitted only in accordance with the principle of first come last go and no discretion or exemptions were allowed. Re-employment of retrenched workmen was provided in order of category-wise seniority if any number of workmen were to be taken in employment within one year.

  Other provisions with respect of issuance of tickets to permanent, temporary and *badli* workers remained the same as in 1960 ordinance as well as the provisions with respect of shift working.

- Leave including Annual Leave with pay, Casual and Sick Leave as provided for under the Factories Act was made applicable to establishments covered by the Standing Orders Ordinance 1968.

SHOPS AND ESTABLISHMENTS ACT

The Weekly Holidays Act 1942 provided for mandatory closing of shops for one day in a week and weekly holiday with pay for every employee. The legislation on shops and establishments in India and Pakistan before 1969 was a provincial subject. Among the State governments, Bombay led the way in 1939 followed by other provinces. The Act contains provisions in respect of opening and closing hours, hours of work, rest interval, spread over, overtime wage and weekly holidays. Some Acts in India provide for an appeal by an employee to the Appropriate Authority against the order of discharge. Despite considerable differences as regards the definitions, the Act broadly covers wage earners employed in shops, commercial establishments including insurance and banking firms, restaurants, theatres, cinemas and other places of public amusement.

The West Pakistan Shops and Establishment Ordinance 1969 replaces the Sindh Shops and Establishments Act 1940, the Punjab Trade Employment Act 1940 and the NWFP Trade

Employees Act 1949 and the Weekly Holidays Act 1942 while protecting the rights and liabilities under these enactments. It provides for weekly holidays in establishments which will remain entirely closed for at least one day in a week and a weekly paid holiday on the day when the establishment is closed. Daily rated and piece rated workers are also entitled to weekly holidays with pay. Weekly hours of work are fixed at nine hours a day and forty-eight hours a week for adults and seven hours a day and forty-two hours a week for young persons. Overtime wages are prescribed at double the ordinary rate of wages but this overtime is not to exceed 150 hours in a year for adults and 100 hours for young workers. Annual leave of fourteen days with pay after continuos employment for a period of twelve months besides casual and sick leave and festival holidays are allowed along the lines as provided for under the Factories Act.

MINES AND MINERALS

Coal Mining is a major industry in India. Conditions of work in this industry were regulated for the first time in 1901, which was replaced by the Indian Mines Act 1923 and then by the Indian Mines Act 1952 and further amended by the Mines (Amendment) Act 1959. The 1952 Mines Act reduced the hours of work both for surface and underground workers to forty-eight hours a week and no worker was allowed to work for more than nine hours a day overground and eighty hours a day underground. The overtime rates which were fixed at one and a half times the ordinary rate of wages for surface workers and twice the same rate for underground workers as earlier was increased to a uniform rate of twice the ordinary rate of wages for both category of coal workers by the 1959 amendment. The employment of women workers underground is prohibited and surface employment was prohibited after 7 p.m. and before 6 a.m. The employment of young persons in the underground work was prohibited in case of those below eighteen, except on a certificate of medical fitness. Annual holidays with pay of fourteen days for monthly paid workers and seven days for weekly paid workers, adults and piece rated workers were promised for.

A Coal Mines Safety and Conservation Fund was created under the Coal Mines Conservation and Safety Act by the imposition of an excise duty on coal mines to assist stoning measures. Under the Coal Mines Labour Welfare Fund Act 1947 a fund was set up to promote the welfare of labour employed in coal mines which was later extended to manganese and mica mines. The Act empowered the Central Government to impose a cess for welfare purposes which included improvement of housing, water supply, educational facilities, recreation, transport and washing facilities.

The Coal Mines Provident Fund and Bonus Act 1948 empowered the government to introduce a provident fund and a bonus scheme for the coal workers.

In Pakistan, mines are not as extensive as in India. The number of workers employed in the industry in Pakistan was only 4526 in 1951. The Indian Mines Act 1923 continued to remain the law. Amendments effecting employment of women underground, reducing the working hours, increasing the rate of overtime to double the ordinary rate of wages were made in 1973 bringing it in line with the amendments made in India in 1952. Similarly, annual leave and holidays with wages were introduced in Pakistan under the Mines Amendment Ordinance 1973. Festival holidays, ten days casual leave and ten days sick leave with pay were also introduced in Pakistan which do not find any place under the Indian Mines Act. In this sphere mines are treated at par with other industrial and commercial establishments covered by the Factories Act in Pakistan.

The definition of minerals has been so modified in India under the 1950 Mines Act so as to specifically include mineral oils, natural gas and petroleum. The Pakistani law does not contain any similar definition and mines have only been defined as any excavation where any operation for the purpose of searching for and obtaining minerals has been or is carried on.

PLANTATION LABOUR ACT 1951 OF INDIA

This Act regulates, for the first time, the conditions of work of plantation workers and provides for their welfare. Though, in the first instance, it applies only to tea, coffee, rubber and cinchona plantations, the State governments have been empowered to extend the provisions of the Act to other plantations with the approval of the Central Government.

The Act fixes a 54-hours week for adults and a 40-hours week for adolescents and children. It prohibits the employment of children under twelve years of age and night work for women and children between the hours 7 p.m. and 6 a.m. and requires medical examination of young persons below eighteen years of age. It also provides for leave with wages for an adult at the rate of one day for every twenty days of work, and for a young person at one day for every fifteen days of work.

Provisions regarding health and welfare, including the appointment of Welfare Officers, are similar to those in the Factories Act, 1948. Provision has also been made requiring every employer to provide and maintain for every worker and his family residing in the plantation the necessary housing accommodation.

The implementation of the Act was held up because of the slump in the tea industry during 1952-53. With the improvement in tea prices, the Act was brought into force from 1 April 1954. The Plantations Labour Ordinance 1962 of Pakistan provides for facilities of drinking water, conservancy medical facilities and canteen, creches, recreational facilities, educational facilities, house building facilities and facilities for daily necessities. Except for drinking water, conservancy, it was left to the government to prescribe by rules the nature and standard of facilities to be provided. Canteen was to be provided for where 150 or more workers were employed and creches where forty or more workmen/women were employed.

Night work for women and children was prohibited and a child who has completed his twelve years and an adolescent who has completed his seventeen years were allowed to work only on the basis of a certificate of fitness. Annual leave with wages for adults at the rate of two days for every thirty days of work performed, for young persons at the rate of one for every twenty days of work performed and five days festival leave with full wages and fifteen days sick leave at half wages were prescribed. Overtime wages were also left to be prescribed by the government.

WORKING JOURNALIST AND NEWSPAPER EMPLOYEES (INDIA)

The Working Journalist (Conditions of Services) and Miscellaneous Provision Act, 1955. In India the Act came into force on 20 December 1955. The most important provisions of the Act concerns the appointment of Wage Boards, their composition, powers, etc. In determining the rates of wages of working journalists, the Board is required to take into consideration the prevailing cost of living and wages in other comparable services for its guidance. Pending a decision by the Board, the government was empowered to fix interim rate of wages. An employer must give six months' notice to an editor and three months' notice to other working journalists in case of retrenchment. Gratuity has to be paid by the employer at the prescribed rates in case of death, retirement, resignation or termination of service. The Employees' Provident Fund Act 1952 and the Industrial Employment (Standing Orders) Act, 1946, have been extended to all newspaper establishments employing twenty working journalists or more. The Act prescribes a maximum of 144 working hours during four consecutive weeks for a journalist. It also contains provision for . a weekly holiday, casual leave, earned leave and leave on medical grounds. Money due to an employee is recoverable from the employer in the same manner as arrears of land revenue. The Working Journalists (Industrial Disputes) Act, 1955, has been repealed and its provisions incorporated in this Act. Decisions of the Wage Board constituted under this Act were set aside by the Supreme Court as being 'illegal and void'.

As a result, an Ordinance was promulgated which was replaced by the Working Journalists' (Fixation of Rates of Wages) Act, 1958. This Act provided for the constitution by the Central Government of a committee to fix rates of wages for working journalists.

These Acts of 1955 and 1958 were amended by the Working Journalists' (Amendment Act, 1962), which mainly provides for:

— the payment of gratuity to a working journalist if he voluntarily resigns on any ground after a total service of ten years and in cases of resignation on grounds of conscience, after a total service of not less than three years;
— the grant of powers to the Central Government to appoint a Wage Board for working journalists, and
— the grant of powers to the State government to appoint Inspectors for the purpose of securing effective implementation of the provisions of the Working Journalist Act.

WORKING JOURNALIST (CONDITIONS OF SERVICE) ORDINANCE XVI OF 1960 (PAKISTAN)

The provisions of Industrial Disputes Ordinance 1959 were made applicable to or in relation to working journalist treating them as workmen within the meaning of that Ordinance. With respect to termination of employment, the working journalists were treated at par with other industrial workers but in case of working journalists, one month's notice or notice pay was required where services were less than three years and two months' notice pay where total period of such service was three years or more.

The establishment of provident fund was made compulsory for every Newspaper Establishment for the benefit of working journalists. The contribution of a working journalist was to begin after the completion of first two years of his service and his contribution was to be not less than 6 per cent and not more than 8 per cent with an equal contribution from the employer. Hours of work were fixed at not more than forty-two hours a week exclusive of the time for meals. Leave was allowed on full wages for not less than $1/11$ for the period spent on duty and medical leave with $1\frac{1}{2}$ of wages for not less than $1/18$th of the period of such service besides ten days casual leave of absence with wages in a calendar year.

A Wage Board may be appointed by a notification for fixing rates of wages in respect of working journalist by a Wage Board consisting of equal number of persons nominated by the Central Government to represent employers in the newspaper establishment and the working journalists.

Standing Orders Ordinance 1960 was made applicable to Newspaper Establishment wherein twenty or more newspaper employees were employed on any day of preceding twelve months.

This Ordinance was repealed and re-enacted as Newspaper Employees (Conditions of Service) Ordinance 1973, making it applicable to journalists as well as non-working journalists. The statement of objectives and reasons is to provide for the following matters, among others:

1. Constitution of Wage Board at the national level for fixing scale of wages in respect of journalists as well as non-journalist newspaper employees.
2. Effective implementation of the decision of the Wage Board.
3. Application of Industrial Relations Ordinance 1969 to all employees.
4. Application of Standing Orders Ordinance 1968 to newspaper establishments employing ten or more workmen.
5. Better welfare measures with respect to security of service, hours of work, leave and medical care.

Every newspaper establishment was required to give an order in writing to the employee at the time of his appointment, transfer or promotion, showing the terms and conditions of his service.

The services of a newspaper employee could not be terminated without good cause shown. A contributory provident fund to which every newspaper employee was required to contribute at least 6½ and not more than 10 per cent of his monthly wages after two years of service with the employer contributing an equal amount. Contribution to the fund could be made by an employee after three months of service with equal contribution from the employer. Provident Funds Act 1925 has been made applicable to the fund created under this law.

The maximum limit of actual working hours for a newspaper employee is fixed at forty-two hours per week excluding time for meals. In other matters the provisions of the Factories Act are applicable such as rest periods, shift working, overtime working and payment thereof.

Annual leave with pay is allowed at the rate of not less than one eleventh of the period spent as duty, Medical leave is permitted at one half of the wage for ¹/₁₈th of the period of service subject to a minimum period of the days in a calendar year and fifteen days casual leave with full wages.

Medical care for a newspaper employee along with his dependents including hospitalization, treatment by a specialist, hospitalization and essential medical supplies as prescribed by the medical practitioner.

Wage Boards could be constituted only for fixing rates of wages and the Board is not competent to decide other terms and conditions of service of newspaper employees. The Wage Board Award is deemed a decision of the full bench of NIRC. A Tribunal is constituted with powers to try an offence for the non-implementation of a decision of Wage Board, to withdraw from any court (except Supreme Court or High Court) any application, proceeding or appeal relating to such offence and dispose of the same. The tribunal has also been given powers to issue a direction for the payment of any amount due to an employee under the Wage Board Award. The Board is authorized to determine the grade of a newspaper and hold an enquiry for the purpose of implementing the Wage Board Award with powers of a Labour Court in adjudicating an industrial dispute.

The 1973 Ordinance was made applicable to all newspaper employees including journalists as well as non-journalists.

FACTORIES AND WORKSHOPS

The Factories Act 1881, was amended several times and in 1934 was overhauled to implement the recommendations of the Royal Commission on Labour in India and the Convention of International Labour Organization. It limited the working hours of the adults to fifty-four in a week and ten hours a day in perennial factories and sixty hours a week in seasonal factories. It provided for a weekly holiday, a rest interval after five hours of continuous work and one and half times ordinary rate of wages for overtime. The ordinary rate of wages was defined to mean wages plus all other allowances. The hours of work for children were restricted to five a day and of women to ten a day and forbade night work for both.

FACTORIES AND WORKSHOP LAWS IN INDIA

In India, the Factories Act 1934 was repealed and re-enacted in 1948 consolidating the law relating to labour in factories which was further amended in 1976. The Act covered all power-using factories employing ten or more workers and non-power using factories employing twenty or more. The Act abolishes the distinction between seasonal and perennial factories. Provisions have been made to safeguard health and promote the safety and welfare of the workers. The minimum age of employment of children has been fixed at fourteen and adolescent person between fifteen to eighteen is allowed to be employed only if medically certified to be fit. The hours of work for adult workers were fixed at forty-eight hours per week and nine hours a day and for children and adolescents a $4^1/_2$ hours day. Adults after completion of one year service are entitled to one day's leave with wages for every twenty days of work and children at the rate of one day's for every fifteen days of work. Extra wages for overtime is to be twice the ordinary rate of wages, inclusive of all allowances except bonus. Spread-over of work is fixed at $10\frac{1}{2}$ hours. Double employment of a worker on any one day in factories is prohibited. Provisions for licensing and registration of factories and prior scrutiny by the Factories Inspectorate of the plans and specification of the factory building has also been included.

FACTORIES AND WORKSHOP LAWS IN PAKISTAN

In Pakistan, wide ranging amendments in the Factories Act 1934 were effected only by Act XVI of 1973. The Act became applicable to all factories employing ten or more workers where manufacturing process was carried on with or without the aid of power. No adult worker is allowed or required to work in a factory for more than forty eight hours a week or nine hours a day in case of perennial factories and fifty hours a week or ten hours a day in a seasonal factory. A 'child' was defined as a person below fifteen years of age and an 'adolescent' as a person who had completed fifteen years but not completed seventeen years of age.

Under section 47-A, the Pakistani Factories Act makes it obligatory for an adult worker to work overtime subject to the provision of the Act and the rules. The Supreme Court had held in 1957-8 that the employer had a right to take overtime from the workers which could not be refused by the workers without sufficient cause. The attention of the Supreme Court of Pakistan does not appear to have been drawn to the fact that even under the then existing law workers were neither permitted to work beyond the stipulated period nor could they be required to do so, unless the exemption clause applied to the specific factory.

Provision with respect to health, safety, welfare, working hours of adults, employment of young persons, annual leave with wages and special provision, display of notices and obligations of workers, are more or less the same under the

Indian and Pakistani Factory Laws, and have been brought up-to-date.

Both in India and Pakistan the government reserves the right to exempt certain factories from any or all of the provisions of the Act. The Indian law empowers the government to exempt workshop or work places attached to a public institution maintained for the purpose of education, training, research or reformation from any or all of the provisions of the Act. The Pakistani law empowers the government including the provincial government to exempt any factory from the provision of this Act in case of public emergency.

Neither the Indian nor the Pakistani law, both of which provide for a compulsory weekly holiday, specifies that it should be with pay. In a number of industrial disputes raised on this count in Pakistan it was held that if weekly holidays were taken into account at the time of fixing wages and dearness allowance, the workers would not be entitled to pay for the weekly holiday. 'Hence in all these cases in which while fixing the daily wages of workmen, the loss of wages to these workmen for Sundays have not been taken into consideration they are entitled to wages for Sundays as well.' (1970 PLC 126-LAT).

RAILWAY SERVANTS HOURS OF EMPLOYMENT REGULATIONS

Until 1930, there was no statutory regulation of the conditions of work of railway servants. By the Indian Railways Amendment Act, 1930, a new chapter was added to the Indian Railway Act, 1890, dealing with hours of work and periods of rest of railway workers. Under the Act, the railway servants hours of employment regulations were framed. Under these regulations, hours of work on railway came to be limited to a maximum of eighty-four a week for persons whose work was declared to be essentially intermittent, and sixty hours a week on an average in any month for others, overtime work allowed under special circumstances being paid for at one-and-a quarter times the ordinary rate of pay. The regulations provided for the granting of periodical rests to certain classes of railway servants whose work was not essentially intermittent. In pursuance of the Award given in 1947 by Justice G.S. Raja Dhyakshe, fresh rules, called the Railway Servants (Hours of Employment) Rules, 1951, were framed. Under these rules the work of all railway servants is divided into four categories, namely (a) intensive, (b) essentially intermittent, (c) excluded, and (d) continuous.

The limits of hours of work fixed are forty-five hours per week for 'intensive' staff, fifty-four hours a week for 'continuous' workers and seventy-five hours per week for 'essentially intermittent' workers. The rules also prescribe that 'intensive' and 'continuous' workers should be given a periodic rest of thirty consecutive hours a week, the 'essentially intermittent' workers a weekly rest of twenty-four consecutive hours including a full night, and 'excluded' workers a rest period of forty-eight consecutive hours in a month or one period of twenty-four consecutive hours in each fortnight. For the running staff, the periodic rest should consist of four periods of at least thirty consecutive hours each or five periods of not less than twenty-two consecutive hours each every month.

Contract labour working for railways, numbering about 700,000, presents yet another problem. Their conditions of service are far from satisfactory and they do not enjoy the privileges given to their fellow workmen in the same industry.

In Pakistan, limitation of employment of railway servants is regulated by Chapter VI A of the Railways Act 1890, as inserted by the Indian Railways Amendment Act 1930. Under these provisions, a railway servant whose employment is not essentially intermittent cannot be employed for more than sixty hours a week on an average in any month, for a railway servant whose work is essentially intermittent the hours are eighty-four in any week.

The West Pakistan Railway Servant Benevolent Fund Ordinance 1969 enacted under the Martial Law Regulations provided for the constitution of a benevolent fund in two parts. Part one for gazetted railway servants which was to consist of compulsory contributions from railway servants at rates determined by the Railway Bar, and grants made by the Railway Board and Pakistan government. The benevolent fund was to be utilized for giving financial assistance to the railway servants.

MOTOR TRANSPORT

The terms and conditions of service for Motor Transport workers in India is regulated by the Motor Transport Workers Act of 1961 and in Pakistan by the Road Transport Workers' Ordinance of 1961, as amended by the Road Transport Workers Amendment Ordinance of 1974. No worker was to be employed for more than forty-eight hours in a week and more than eight hours a day. Rest interval of half an hour before five hours work at a time and two half hourly intervals where he had worked for seven hours. Annual leave with full pay for fourteen days in case of continuous employment of twelve months and not less than seven days leave with full pay in case of employment for six months. Twelve days festival holiday with full pay in a year. Ten days casual leave on full wages.

The provisions of West Pakistan Industrial and Commercial Employment Standing Orders Ordinance 1968 was made applicable to Motor Transport Service in respect of group insurance (only those employing more than forty-nine workers), bonus payable in Motor Transport Service employing more than nineteen, gratuity was payable for service after 27 September 1974 to Motor Transport Service employing more than nineteen workers. Remedy against termination, retrenchment and dismissal was available like the workers covered under the Standing Orders Ordinance and reasons in writing had to be given for termination to workers covered by the provisions of the Standing Order 15 of 1968.

However, road transport workers employed by the Road Transport Corporation were subjected to the removal of Undesirable Employees Ordinance 1965, where an employee, considered to be an undesirable person by the Competent

Authority could be removed only by giving a show cause with a right of appeal to the government. Gratuity and provident fund if admissible was payable if so ordered.

The Law on Sales Promotion Employees (The Sales Promotion Employees Conditions of Services) Act 1976 (India)

The law applied to sales promotion employees engaged in any establishment for hire or reward to do any work, relating to promotion of sales or business or both. Establishment meant under this law to be an establishment engaged in pharmaceutical or any notified industry.

The provisions of Industrial Disputes Act 1947, the Minimum Wages Act 1948, the Maternity Benefit Act 1961, the Payment of Bonus Act 1965, the Payment of Gratuity Act 1972 and the Workmen's Compensation Act 1923 were made applicable to the sales promotion employees drawing wages or commission equal to Rs. 750 per month or 9,000 per annum.

The Act also extended facilities of earned leave on full wages and leave on medical certificate, besides casual leave or other kind of prescribed lien, wages for weekly rest and on all holidays and compensatory holidays.

The Act in India has met a long standing requirement since sales employees/representative were long denied the benefits of various labour laws and the courts both in India and Pakistan had held that sales representatives were not workmen, doing manual, skilled or unskilled or clerical work. Similar legislation may be required to be enacted in Pakistan also.

17 THE LAWS OF SPECIAL GROUPS

Under the bonded labour system, the landlord advances loan in cash or kind or permits the agricultural labourer to occupy as homestead land owned by the landlord in lieu of which the latter becomes bonded to render service to the landlord and to no one else, at nominal wages or for no wage at all till the loan is repaid. In most cases this turns into life-long bondage and passes on to the heirs of the agricultural labourer. This in actual fact is the continuation of the system of serfdom and the advancement of loan is a pretext in most cases and with usurious compound rate of interest, serves to keep the agricultural labourer in life-long bondage.

In India, the Bonded Labour System (Abolition) Ordinance 1975 replaced by an Act of 1976, abolishes the bonded labour system and frees every bonded labourer. The Act prohibits any person from making any advance under the bonded labour system or compelling any person to render bonded labour or any other form of forced labour. Any custom, tradition or any other contract, agreement or other instrument, whether entered into or executed before or after the Act, requiring any person to perform bonded labour was declared null and void. At the same time every obligation of a bonded labourer to repay any bonded debt before or after the passing of the Act became extinguished. Eviction from any homestead or residential premises occupied by the bonded labourer before the commencement of the Act is also prohibited.

THE LAW OF BONDED LABOUR

In Pakistan Bonded Labour System (Abolition) Act 1992 prohibits the making of and declares as void and inoperative any contract, agreement, instrument, custom or tradition or practice by virtue of which any person or member of his family is required to do any work or render any service as a bonded labourer, under the bonded labour system.

The bonded labour system has been defined under the law as a system where:

> In consideration of a *peshgi* advance received by him or any member of his family, a person by himself or through any member of his family renders labour or service either without wages or for nominal wages or forfeits freedom of employment with any other person for a specified or non-specified period or forfeits the right to freely move from one place to another or forfeit the right to appropriate or sell at the market price his property and includes a surety who agrees to render bonded service on the failure of the debtor and on his behalf.

The law declares all such agreements or liabilities undertaken before the commencement of the Act as having been extinguished and even sales and transfers of property of a bonded labourer for recovery of bonded debt is declared ineffective and provision made for the restoration of the property to the debtor.

However, the provisions of law reveal the extent of the prevalence of bonded labour slavery, more than the efficacy of the remedy or the relief granted by it. NGOs in Sindh have in the recent past succeeded in freeing bonded peasant labourers from the private jails of the *Waderas* but the penal provisions of the Bonded Labour Act or even the ordinary law could not be invoked against the tormentors of bonded labourers. In some cases the freedom gained by these bonded labourers have proved to be temporary and the power of the landlords succeeded in throwing them again into dungeons reminding one of the medieval barbarism existing in Pakistan even today.

A recent memorandum of the Human Rights Commission to the Governor of Sindh throws some light on the unsolved problem of Bonded Labour which is essentially the problem of social economic emancipation from a medieval bondage continuing in the twenty-first century.

THE LAW ON CHILD LABOUR

The issue of child labour in the developing countries, including India and Pakistan, has assumed some considerable importance in recent times, both nationally and internationally. Though it may be argued that the concern shown towards the problem of child labour by the developed countries in the name of human rights is not always genuine and too often motivated by fear of competition from cheap labour, the fact remains that under the economic condition in India and Pakistan, children are being denied basic rights of being children, who could play, enjoy and study and live their own carefree and innocent lives. It is universally recognized that no enlightened nation can afford to leave the question of child's welfare to chance or to compulsions of domestic economic requirement.

The International Labour Organization has defined child labour as:

> Child Labour includes children prematurely leading adult lives, working long hours for low wages, under conditions damaging to their health and to their physical and mental development sometimes separated from their families, frequently deprived of meaningful education and training opportunities that could open up for them a better future. These include children working in any section, occupation or process including the formal and non-formal, organized and unorganized within or outside the family.

The Apprenticeship Act 1850 enabled the pledging of Indian children between the age of ten and fourteen years for a period not exceeding seven years or until he reached the age of twenty years on payment of a paltry sum to the parents. What is more, the pledging under an apprenticeship agreement was enforceable through a Magistrate who was empowered to impose a penalty for the breach of the so-called Apprenticeship Agreement. Under the Apprenticeship Agreement no wages were payable to the apprentices until they reached the age of adulthood. This law remained on the statute book till 1933, when under The Children (Pledging of Labour) Act 1933 the parent or guardian of a child (under the age of fifteen) was prohibited from entering into an agreement in return of payments received or to be received for allowing the services of a child to be utilized in any employment. However, an agreement could be made for allowing a child to be employed for reasonable wages, which agreement could be terminated on a week's notice. Thus, child labour was not prohibited even under the 1933 Act. Only pledging was prohibited. Under the Constitution of the Indian Republic, a person below the age of 14 years is defined as a child.

The ILO estimate puts the number of working children throughout the world between the ages of five and fourteen to nearly 250 million out of which 120 million work whole time and at least one third in hazardous occupations.

In South Asia 'several tens of millions' of child labourer are exploited by slavery and forced labour system, the most common of which is debt bondage in which children are forced to work to pay off a debt or other obligation incurred by the family.

Estimates computed on the basis of families being below poverty line puts that figure of child labour in India at 77 million according to the Commission on Labour Standard and International Trades Government of India 1995.

The Factories Act 1948 raised the minimum age of employment in factories to fourteen years, so did the Employment of Children (Amendment) Act 1949, and the Apprenticeship Act 1961. Employment of Children (Amendment) Act 1978 prohibited employment of children below fifteen years in railway premises, building operations, in catering establishments or in work in close proximity of railway lines. The Child Labour (Prohibition and Regulation) Act 1986 prohibited the employment of children in seven occupations and eighteen processes listed in the schedule for person below fourteen years of age. The Plantation Labour Act prohibited the employment of children under twelve years of age. Under the

Mines Act 1952 children under fifteen were prohibited from being employed in the mines. For underground the age limit was raised to sixteen years with the requirement of a certificate of medical fitness. Persons under seventeen were prohibited from employment during night hours in a factory by the Factories (Amendment) Act 1954. The Merchant Shipping Act 1958 and the Motor Transport Workers Act 1961 raised the age to fifteen years under which employment was prohibited.

In Pakistan, employment of children is regulated by the provisions of the Employment of Children Act 1992. Persons below the age of fourteen in scheduled employment or processes which include beedi-making, carpet-weaving, cloth-printing, dyeing and weaving, matches, explosives and fireworks besides mica-cutting and splitting etc., and manufactures using toxic materials such as mercury, manganese etc.

Both in India and Pakistan, a proviso in the laws for abolition of child labour in hazardous industries exempts child labour belonging to the family of the employer. This leaves a loophole and is often misused by the employers.

Despite a plethora of legislation on the subject in both the countries, the most recent ones being enacted under international pressure, there are great doubts about their efficacy given the high rates of illiteracy, unemployment and massive poverty. The provisions of law are more likely to remain merely on the statute book. The example of the province of Kerala in India would probably indicate the real causes of the evil of child labour as well as the factors which can help eradicate it. In Kerala, the percentage of literacy is as high as above 90 per cent and the incidence of child labour is also extremely low.

The statute law does not really touch upon the problem of child labour and its abolition because there are thousands beyond the pale of laws and its implementation machinery. The problem is primarily of absolute grinding poverty which forces child labours to be sucked in the industrial machinery. Child labour may be abolished in such industries as carpet-weaving, wool scouring, the sports goods industry, the beedi-industry, etc. The government, forced by threats of economic boycott of goods manufactured with the help of child labour may act on an occasion or two supported by publicity fanfares. But the evil only goes underground or is dispersed, often passed off as 'informalization' of industry. Though the problem of abolition of child labour has to be addressed separately which cannot wait till the total transformation of society, it cannot be separated from the struggle to eradicate poverty in the Third World countries.

LEGISLATION CONCERNING WORKING WOMEN

Equal Remuneration Act 1976 was enacted in India on 11 February 1976 which gave statutory effect to the internationally recognized principles of payment of remuneration at equal rate to men and women workers providing that no employer shall pay to any worker employed by him/her in an establishment or employment less remuneration than paid by him/her to the workers of the opposite sex performing the same work or work of a similar nature. The Act shall come into force on dates appointed by the Central Government for different establishments for employment but not later than three years from passing of the Act. Another provision of the Act prohibited any discrimination against women in respect of making recruitment for the same work or work of similar nature where employment of women was not prohibited under any law. An Advisory Committee for the purpose of providing increasing employment opportunity for women was to be appointed which was to be composed of not less than ten persons of which half were to be women. Appropriate government was required to appoint officers to hear complaints with regard to the contravention of any provision of this Act or claims arising out of non-payment of wages under the Act. However, terms and conditions relating to retirement, marriage or death were not be effected by the law of equal treatment for men and women.

In Pakistan there is no special law containing the provisions of the above universally recognized principles of equal remuneration for equal work. Certain recommendations with respect to working women and their needs were made by a Commission, which suggested the creation of a non-discriminatory system of laws disavowing reliance on gender as a classificatory devise. All existing labour legislation and new legislation was recommended to be drafted with a firm commitment to the rejection of gender as a classificatory device.

The exclusion of some sectors of economy such as agriculture was noted as likely to leave working women unprotected. Some other sectors where banning of trade union activities particularly effected the women workers adversely were also noticed such as Pakistan Security Printing Corporation, the Ministry of Defence, the Export Processing Zone and Special Industrial Zone, etc. In respect of Workmen's Compensation Act it was recommended that the provision with respect to women's receipt of compensatory payment should be deleted. It was recommended that women should be compensated on the internationally recognized principles of equal pay for equal work. A special minimum quota should be fixed for apprenticeship for women in order to ensure that they have access to training facilities. Additional work place security, strict penalties for sexual harassment as well as other crimes against women and un-reluctant enforcement to protect working women was recommended.

There were other recommendations with respect to the representation of women on the executive committees of the trade unions, commensurate with the percentage of the work force that they comprise in the establishment. Discrimination was noted in the Employees Old Age Benefit Act 1976 where it provided for survivors pension in case of a male child until he attains eighteen years of age and in case of a female child until she attains eighteen years of age or until marriage whichever is earlier. It was recommended that the survivors' pension should be given to all children male or female till they attain age of twenty-one. The Committee recommended the addition of agricultural and domestic workers into the definition of workers in order to bring them within the purview of all law applying thereto. But the recommendation of this Commission has not yet taken a form of any statutory provision.

18 LOOKING INTO THE FUTURE

State intervention and regulation of what may be called the labour market in the Indian subcontinent began in the early stages of imperial dominated economy itself. In British-owned tea plantations and the collieries where labour was not available or was not easily attracted because of arduous working conditions and great distances from the populated areas, resort was had to indentured labour through severe penal provisions. Besides the forced labour camps in the tea plantation in the early part of the century, there were the Gorakhpuri labour camps in the coal field of Jharia, Dhanbad (Bihar) and Asansol, during the Second World War; virtual slave camps where labour signed away its freedom under a so called free contract, were not allowed to go out of the camps except under escort on week days and whose wages were withheld for payment of food and board and the balance paid at the end of the contract period if at all.

Thus, even in an under-developed economy like India's with a labour surplus market in general, specific segments like coal mining and plantation experienced labour shortage. In these conditions State intervention did not come about in the first instance as 'welfarism' but in the form of imposing slave-like conditions generally associated with indentured labour. Forms of 'debt slavery' are prevalent even today not only amongst agricultural labour, who, in many cases, were found to be kept in chains alongwith the members of their families in the interior of Sindh. Then there are the ill-reputed *Kharkar* Camps. Similar labour bondage also widely prevailed among brick-klins workers in Punjab in Pakistan and parts of India. Ironically enough, this labour bondage system was sometimes justified in the name of sanctity of contract under Islam. Child slave labour was sanctioned in the early years of British rule under the law which not only permitted pledging of children for work in the factories on payment of paltry amounts to their parents but made violation of these pledges criminally punishable. It was only later that pledging of child labour was abolished sometimes in 1933.

It was with the advent of political reforms, the gradual strengthening of the movement for democracy, the consciousness of the national movement in general and the trade union movement in particular, that labour laws began to be enacted which provided some relief to the extreme exploitation of the industrial working class under the British rule. The labour laws became a little humanized.

The law on trade union which was introduced in 1926 for the first time in India was a double-edged sword. It prohibited political strikes nicknamed as '*hartals*' at the same time that it recognized the right of workers to form trade unions free of the threat of damages for breach of contract. The law recognizing the right of association of trade unions came about in the back ground of the Soviet Socialist revolution and also of the British general strike of 1926.

The Whitley Commission report and the acceptance of some of its recommendation by the British government coincided with a change in the political situation in India and the introduction of provincial autonomy and popularly elected governments in the provinces under the Government of India Act 1935.

Corresponding to the political vicissitudes which Pakistan had been passing through since independence, four broad periods can be noted in the labour relations policy of the succeeding regimes and the labour laws introduced by them. The first corresponds to the achievement of political independence and the foundation of the State up to the first martial law. The second to the period under Ayub Khan which was euphemistically called the 'glorious decade'. The third period could be conveniently split into two sub-periods between 1968-72 and 1972-7. The fourth period beginning from the long martial law period of General Ziaul Haq between 1977-88 can be said to reluctantly continue the earlier labour legislation with emphasis on taking out larger segments of industries and establishments from the application of laws of industrial dispute and trade union legislation. This policy is being further carried forward under the present regime with greater thrust.

The pre-independence framework of labour laws, carried into the first post-independence decade both in India and Pakistan could be best described as one of minimal State interference in the field of employment conditions and a strict control over strikes breaking out in public utility services. It corresponded to the classical *laissez faire* policy but did not leave the matter to be entirely determined by the free interplay of market forces or the bargaining strength of the respective sides. It did not set out to determine by statute the minimum terms and conditions of industrial or commercial employment but stepped in when things got out of hand to set up an adjudicatory process.

In India, industrial establishments were left free to work out their own 'standing orders' and specific terms and conditions of service, subject to their being certified by the certifying authority after inviting objections from the trade unions and the workers. The machinery provided for the settlement of contesting claims of the employers and the workers in an industry through industrial actions like strikes or lock-outs. The government had the power to intervene when strikes or lock-outs got out of hand and a reference was then made to industrial adjudication, which were few and far between, entirely depending upon the discretion of the government when 'public interest' demanded it. A distinction was made between public utility concerns and non-public utility concerns and in the latter government interference was still less forthcoming. In India, ameliorative statutory measures have been minimal except for Social Security legislation and the regulation of employer's right to hire and fire, lay-off or close down the establishment.

In Pakistan, industrial adjudication became almost compulsory and Industrial Courts became a part of a permanent judicial system replacing collective bargaining during the 'glorious decade'. There were still no significant statutory determination of the terms and conditions of industrial employment. They were left to be determined by the Industrial

Courts only when industrial disputes arose in individual cases. The 1960 Standing Orders Ordinance in Pakistan did not add much to the liability of the industrial employer.

STATUTORY DETERMINATION OF TERMS OF EMPLOYMENT

State intervention in the realm of statutory determination of the minimum terms and conditions of industrial and commercial employment in Pakistan came in the wake of the socio-political upheavals towards the end of the decade of the first martial law. The minimum wages ordinance putting the minimum wages at Rs. 140 per month for unskilled labour in 1969, the Standing Orders Ordinance 1968 introducing Compulsory Gratuity Scheme, the Companies Profits (Workers Participation) Act 1968 and the Social Security enactment of 1965 were some of the more significant measures taking State intervention into a different sphere from the earlier period. In the period 1972-73, other measures followed, introducing a compulsory Group Insurance Scheme, a Profit Bonus Scheme, enhancing the rate of gratuity made payable also on resignation and also abolition of workers' contribution in the Social Security Scheme and the enhancement of leave available to industrial workers by way of casual leave and sick leave, besides annual leave. Then there was the Workers' Children Education Cess and ultimately the Employees Old Age Benefit Scheme. Altogether an impressive array of beneficial legislation.

The Industrial Relations Ordinance 1969 in Pakistan divided the matters of dispute in industries as those pertaining to rights secured or guaranteed under the law, settlement or award and matters of interest left to be determined by means of collective bargaining between the employers and the worker. The policy of law was to determine more and more disputed questions between workers and employers by means of the statutory provision and therefore enforceable only through law courts and leave less and less for a trial of strength between the contending parties. Since 1973, the question of Dearness Allowance and compensation for the rising spiral of high prices has also been taken care of by the Cost of Living Relief Act though not under any formula nor at regular intervals and the minimum Cost of Living Allowance under the statute worked out to be Rs. 150 per month by 1985. By now the minimum wages for unskilled workmen come to Rs. 2050 under the statute including the Cost of Living Allowance and various other special allowances. In step with these statutory determination of the terms and conditions of employment, State interference has proceeded apace not only in respect of the manner in which trade unions resort to industrial action. State control and regulations extend to the management of the internal affairs of the unions including elections of their office bearers and raising of industrial disputes. Not every registered trade union could now raise an industrial dispute. The concept and practice of an elected collective bargaining agent was introduced.

SPHERES OF STATE INTERFERENCE

State interference, regulation and control in the matter of industrial relations and minimum terms of employment thus extends today to three distinct spheres, which may be termed as regulatory, beneficial and supervisory. Regulatory intervention in so far as it strictly lays down the limits within which strike actions/lock-outs can be resorted to, the procedure which has to be strictly followed and the conditions under which strikes or lock-outs can be altogether prohibited and the dispute seized by the Labour Courts. Beneficial in so far as the minimum terms and conditions of employment from wages to the fringe benefits are determined by law and supervisory to the extent that the internal management of the trade unions and the elections of collective bargaining agent are supervised and/or conducted by government agencies.

It can very well be said that the sphere of State interference in industrial relations under the mandatory and statutory provisions in Pakistan is much more comprehensive than in India and probably more than most of the developing countries. The policies of privatization and liberalization being actively followed in the field of industries during the succeeding regimes of both Benazir Bhutto and Nawaz Sharif have resulted in the so-called welfare legislations taking a back seat and now being relegated to the restrictive laws applicable to labour and the trade unions.

STRUCTURAL REFORMS AND LIBERALIZATION

The present stage in the economic policies of both the countries of India and Pakistan are expressed in the phraseology of ascendant world capitalism, structural reforms, liberalization and globalization of world trade. Shorn of new and misleading terminology, it represents the theory of unregulated marketization, attaching a sort of sanctity to the working of market mechanism instead of planning and State direction. In terms of labour policy this would probably mean a minimal labour legislation and gradual abandonment of welfare and protective measures.

The immediate impact of these policies in the field of employment conditions has been massive downsizing, almost total retrenchment of the old work force manning nationalized industries on their privatization and their substitution by casual labour. In Pakistan the means adopted for overcoming resistance to the consequences of these policies has been to take out the matter from the ambit of jurisdiction of the Labour Courts and by a deeming clause in the Federal Services Tribunal Act, transforming the industrial workers of State owned or controlled Industries into 'civil servants' whose terms and conditions of service became the exclusive jurisdiction of the Civil Services Tribunal by virtue of section 2-A in the Federal Services Tribunal Act. An amendment in banking laws saddled the functioning of trade unions in the banking industry with numerous conditions.

Another method adopted in Pakistan to soften the resistance to privatization and denationalization of industries coupled with massive retrenchment was to offer a 'Golden Handshake' Scheme and offering the workers a preferential treatment in the purchase of shares in the privatized industries. The 'golden handshake scheme' with specific variations offered 'separation benefits' in addition to and considerably higher than gratuity benefits on retirement. Most of the workers having opted for this 'Golden Handshake', it was found to be uneconomical so that the scheme was not pursued in the subsequent privatization of industries which was to follow the initial handing over of management to private parties.

The scheme of workers or employees management groups purchasing the majority shares offered and taking over management in some privatized industries does not appear to have succeeded in Pakistan and in consequence the provident and gratuity fund of the workers utilized for this purpose have evaporated or lost much of its value in the collapse of the Stock Exchange during the last four or five years. The trade unions in India were better informed when they foresaw this as the effect of stock exchange fluctuations on the workers share and rejected any so-called workers take over in competition with multi-nationals.

Structural adjustment is about making the economy 'market friendly'. It is in this context that labour laws are increasingly looked upon as a costly nuisance, brought into being as measures of cheap populism, harming if not altogether sacrificing 'investment and development' at the alter of expediency so that according to the perceptions of the policy-makers, the sooner these labour laws are swept away the better it is. But they would still like to retain State control and regulation in the sphere of industrial dispute mechanism and in the formation and functioning of trade unions, and only do away or minimize the State intervention in the matter of determining the minimum terms and conditions of service and social security measures.

So like the 'glorious decade' in Pakistan, once again there is the growing trend of giving priority to development over social justice and equity on the ground that 'incentives' are necessary for investment, both foreign and domestic. The comments of a chairman of pre-independence National Planning Committee of Indian National Congress may be still relevant in this respect.

> No one quite seems to realize that the incentives of the classes may by themselves prove to be disincentive for the masses and what we need is a complex of incentives that will motivate both the classes and the masses to play their proper role in speeding the tempo of development. There can be no massive development without the masses active and positive participation in the process of economic growth.

THE EFFECTS OF GLOBALIZATION

At the turn of century, the economic policies hitherto followed in South Asian countries namely the policies of a mixed economy, with the State sector providing the sinews for an autonomous and self-reliant industrial development, are being given a go by. The euphoria is spread that the universalization of free market economy through globalization, restructuring and liberalization, would succeed in enabling the Third World countries to enter into an era of prosperity and development and therefore an end to trade unionism and labour laws is on the agenda. The long-term effect of these policies would require a separate space and discussion. Here we are directly concerned with the effects of these policies and that of 'globalization' of world trade on what may be termed as the laws governing the labour sector of the economy or the labour market.

Terminologies like export-oriented economy in place of 'import substitution' economy, liberalization etc. often serve to conceal the main thrust of the changes being envisaged in directing the economic scenario. In Pakistan, while import tariffs are drastically reduced, opening up the local market to the invasion of multi-nationals, general sales tax increases the cost of local manufacture leading up to the process of de-industrialization of the country. What also appears, to be agreed upon by analysts of globalization is that trade union rights and with them the 'liberal' or 'welfare-oriented' labour laws are out of order in the new dispensation. It is argued that the hey days of labour legislation coincided with 'Statism' which is now a matter of the past, and only a decent burial awaits the 'populist' or 'welfare'-oriented labour laws. That these laws constitute an unwholesome burden on the industry and its capacity to compete in the open market with the multi-nationals is the battle cry of the new economist. It is also claimed that 'labour movement could reap considerable benefits as long as import substitution industrialization strategy provided protection and predictability in the domestic market,' that trade unions were able to build powerful position in collective bargaining in parastatal enterprises resulting in 'over-employment' and unreasonable wage structures not justified by market functioning. This assumption is however not justified by the history of labour laws.

The history of labour laws both before and after independence indicates that the main factor behind their being put on the statute book was the desire to avoid a serious outbreak of social and political discontent, as a part of the strategy of social and economic management. If the State, through mechanism of regulatory laws, softened the impact of industrial conflict inherent in a developing industrial society, it had also to step in to provide minimum guarantees of remuneration and social security by law to act as a cushion against the cruel working of purely market forces. If a free fall of market mechanism is allowed to determine the price of labour, there would not be any justification left not to allow free hand to labour to use the mechanism of collective bargaining in determining those prices. It is a historical fallacy to associate the strength of collective bargaining of organized labour with the development of 'Statism' or the public sector in economy. State intervention in India and Pakistan in both fields—regulating and minimizing industrial disputes and that of regulating the labour market and the working conditions in the industry so as to minimize serious disputes—have been part of the same policy pattern in the developing economics of the Third World.

The multinationals are entering the market of the developing nations also through the strength of their technology which is said to have significantly cut back the manufacturing jobs in France, Japan, the UK and the USA. There are forecasts predicting that 10 per cent of the work-force might be able to produce all the material needs of the population by the twenty-first century. This technology has not yet arrived in India and Pakistan but the policy-makers here appear to be making up the deficiency in their own technological development by following an open door policy to foreign investors and providing them with a 'union free' and 'cheap labour' market. We have seen in Pakistan how the exemption of more than 50 per cent of the labour force in industries and other establishments from the industrial relations laws has already created a 'union free' zone of industries. The process of keeping wage rises in check has been initiated by a suggestion in the policy paper of Government of Pakistan to reduce the overtime payment from 'double the ordinary rate of pay' to one and a half times, to virtually abolish the annual leave and other leaves with pay in lieu of 'encashment' and to appoint a 'wage-fixing authority' to determine and fix wages of all categories of workers.

The massive downsizing taking place in the banking and other financial institutions as well as in the privatized industries at least in Pakistan is not the result of an introduction of new technology but as a response to alleged over-employment of previous regimes. It is doubtful if the downsizing is likely to result in any cut down in costs, since the banking institutions are said to be over-burdened with 'feudal levies' in the form of massive political loans to big feudal lords who matter in the enclaves of power which are unrealizable and add to the cost of industry.

THE GROWTH OF INFORMAL SECTOR

A part of the same strategy of market economy both in India and Pakistan is the growth of the informal sector or rather the 'informalization' of the organized sector through mechanism of contract system, which poses new challenges to the trade unions and to the administration of labour laws with respect to the security of service, social security and minimum terms of employment. The present government in Pakistan, with its proposals of 'flexibility' in the labour relations and striking a *via media* between security of service and the power 'to hire and fire,' is trying to reverse the protection hitherto provided by the labour laws even in certain restricted sphere. While in India, the law of contract labour 1970, provides a welcome protection to labour in this field, yet the discretionary powers of the Government in the matter of abolition of contract labour, leaves such a vast industrial establishment as the Tata Iron and Steel Company free to run its steel mills in very considerable part with the employment of contract labour.

In Pakistan, we have noticed the state and policy of law with respect to the introduction of contract labour. Now we have the prospect of official patronage extended to the system on the plea that it has become too widespread in industries to be abolished. It may however be quite important to distinguish the 'contract labour system' in India and Pakistan with the 'contracting-out of work' associated with the introduction of latest technologies in countries like Japan. While even in the case of the latter the aim and the result of the contract system transforming employees into self-employed persons, is to deprive the workers of the legally-based protection that the status of a 'worker' or an employee carries, namely the protection of an award, and a union negotiated settlement and even of statute-law. As 'contracted' labour, even in advanced industrialized countries, it would mean for the worker turned into his own employer paying his own insurance, workers' compensation and possibly superannuation without his annual and sick leave. Here in Pakistan and India, most of the 'contract labour' is performed in the same factory premises, on the same machines and the same work environment as well as with the same raw material as the rest of the workers and it is only the company supervisor who now dons the robe of a 'contractor' employing 'his own' labour. It is only the 'fig leaf' of a formal contract which hides the naked truth of blatant legal manoeuvres to circumvent the application of labor laws.

For the time, it therefore appears that while the industrialized West is fast developing breathtaking new technologies, our countries are still beset with the strategy of reducing cost by reducing wages and other benefits in order to attract foreign investment and also to 'compete' with the West in producing cheaper goods for the export market. The dominating perception appears to be that the industrial laws in so far as they provide a minimum guaranteed wages, social security, gratuity and bonus should be watered-down or done away with and the laws controlling, curtailing or prohibiting the law of industrial disputes and collective bargaining be made more stringent. It is the regime of one way free enterprise which many of the policy-makers would like to prevail in both the countries.

It is often argued that protective and beneficial labour laws merit to be discarded at the altar of globalization because with globalization a lot of foreign capital is likely to be attracted and a lot of investment will take place. Better to reduce wages and labour standards in order to achieve higher employment. But there are valid grounds to believe that what is happening is not globalization of productive capital but globalization of finance, which was behind the 'collapse' of the tiger economies and of the Stock Exchange in Pakistan.

Downsizing referred to earlier has been carried out in a massive way in all the major financial institutions, industries and newspaper industries in Pakistan without any well-thought and worked-out scheme of rationalization. There has been nothing like the agreement between the Indian Bankers' Association on the one side and the All India Bank Employees Association and the National Confederation of Bank Employees, as far back as September 1983 limiting the extent of mechanization in the banks. Maintenance of the existing work force and new recruitment commensurate with the expansion of the banking industry were some of the other important features of the agreement.

New challenges and complex problems of managing technological changes are rising in all countries because of severe insufficiencies and imbalances in the present day social and economic organization. The basic question which continues to be posed is who controls it, to what purpose, for whom and against whom. Techonological changes can neither be resisted nor should they be. In fact, the need of the developing countries is transfer of technology with the investment of foreign capital. The role of the State shall continue to be decisive in determining the direction of development and the fields where foreign capital is most needed.

The conclusions which can be drawn in the context of the present review is that economic regeneration and development cannot succeed on the basis of massive unemployment and denial of basic minimum requirement of health, education and a minimum living wage. The overall development strategy has to evolve a socially-oriented policy. The future of labour laws depends on which policy is ultimately adopted in India and Pakistan as part of their development strategies in the twenty-first century.

The continued necessity of labour laws guaranteeing the minimum terms and conditions of employment is underlined by the hue and cry raised by the trade unions of developed western countries, particularly USA against what is being termed as 'social dumping' and for introducing International Labour Standards before free imports or before the lowering of tariffs is allowed in respect of import of manufactured goods from the developing countries. It reminds one of the historical similarities with the situation when Lancashire workers demonstrated against long working hours in the unregulated textile factories of Bombay and elsewhere in India. The motivations today may be as selfish for the workers of the developed countries of the West. But the aim of the trade unions in both the developed and developing countries would continue to be to prevent a slump in labour standards following globalization.

SELF-RELIANCE AND THE ROLE OF ·THE TRADE UNION MOVEMENT

The role of trade union movement assumes a new significance in India and Pakistan in the context of the struggle which is bound to develop in these countries for national self-reliance and all round social and economic development. Globalization based on the technological superiority of the West, which is able to impose itself on the still feudal dominated and debt ridden economics with over-burdened militarization, is not likely to solve the problems of poverty with a system of unbridled and rapacious capitalism.

Trade union movement in the subcontinent had always been invested, in a greater or lesser degree with moral and political aspiration, partaking of a national character and not merely concerned with the question of higher wages and better living conditions, because there was a patent relationship with the socio-political setup at a given point. Links between the socio-economics demands of the working class, a general concept of social justice and egalitarian socialism and the aims and perspective of the national movement had always inspired the early pioneers of the trade union movement. Even though dimmed at present particularly since the demise of socialist state system in European countries, the objectives and motivation have not lost their relevance. John Strachey, in his well-known work *Development of Capitalism* has cogently drawn attention to the historical phenomena of capitalism's inherent tendency to depress working class conditions being checked and even reversed only by the strength of the trade union movement and the ideas of socialism. So one has to be on guard both on the national and trade union plane as the twenty-first century dawns. The new labour management technique now includes a conscious policy of corrupting the trade union leadership, creating specially patronized trade union bureaucracy with exemption from normal plant duties and provision of perks and facilities reserved for senior management officials. A parallel to the application of the same techniques to governmental and administrative bureaucracy in the developing countries is not very difficult to find with abounding instances of corruption at the level of multi-national economic relationships and at the national level of special privilege groups having at their disposal the resources of nationalized banks and financial institutions, at the same time that fiscal and taxation policies are mouded in the interest and at the dictation of international power brokers.

The end of history can only be predicated on the end of the struggle of the classes, of the 'haves' and 'have nots' together with an end to national and ethnic conflict. An end to the first can come about probably only in an economy of super abundance in which personal greed and imperial domination lose their relevance and necessity. But before that, an arduous and prolonged struggle awaits the long-suffering working humanity to drag itself out of the overwhelming and abysmal degradation of poverty, squalor and ignorance. Not the 'end of man' but the 'empowerment of man' is what the new millennium may look forward to.

INDEX